'As a counsellor, reading this updated version of *You Can Change* is refreshing. I'm in the business of helping people to change, but often, people lack clarity on exactly what needs to change and how (and how long it might take!). Tim's book gives clear, practical guidance that brings Jesus to the forefront, reminding us that it is only by his power that we become more like him. This book is full of grace and hope. I highly recommend it!'
Kristin L. Kellen, Associate Professor of Biblical Counseling, Southeastern Baptist Theological Seminary

'Fifteen years ago, the first edition of this super book was a great help to me: its content has been significant in my own progress towards holiness; and it has helped shaped much of my pastoral approach to the same subject as I have the privilege of a front-row seat in people's lives. It is still needed, not least because of the unchanging spiritual battles we all face. In fact, I think the need now is greater and this revised volume keeps the content fresh and applies it in new and helpful directions that resonate with today's challenges. Tim writes as a fellow traveller first, pastor second – but it is the unique combination of this self-awareness, honesty and spiritual hopefulness that makes reading and rereading worthwhile. Here you will find pastoral carefulness and historical insight, all filtered through the lens of biblical faithfulness, from the pen of one of our finest Christian authors.'
Adrian Reynolds, pastor, author and Head of National Ministries, Fellowship of Independent Evangelical Churches, UK

Tim Chester is a senior faculty member of Crosslands Training and the author of more than forty books. He has a PhD in theology and twenty-five years' experience of pastoral ministry. He is married with two grown-up daughters and lives in rural Derbyshire where he is part of a church plant.

YOU CAN CHANGE

God's transforming power for our sinful
behaviour and negative emotions

Second edition

Tim Chester

INTER-VARSITY PRESS
SPCK Group, Studio 101, The Record Hall, 16–16A Baldwin's Gardens, London
EC1N 7RJ, England
Email: ivp@ivpbooks.com
Website: www.ivpbooks.com

© Tim Chester, 2008, 2024

First published 2008
Second edition 2024

British Library Cataloguing-in-Publication Data
A catalogue record for this book is available from the British Library.

ISBN: 978–1–78974–493–4
eBook ISBN: 978–1–78974–494–1

Set in 11/14 pt Minion Pro
Typeset in Great Britain by Fakenham Prepress Solutions, Fakenham, Norfolk
NR21 8NL
Printed and bound in Great Britain by Clays Ltd, Elcograf S.p.A.

Produced on paper from sustainable sources

Contents

Preface to second edition

It's fifteen years since *You Can Change* was first published. In that time I've benefited hugely from talking with the readers I've met around the world. My ongoing pastoral involvement and inter-action with students, especially with my Crosslands students, has continued to clarify my thinking. I've also read a number of helpful new books that have been published in that time.

It's also been fifteen years of change for me. I've grown in my understanding of the gospel and my appreciation of Jesus. Some of that change has come from my studies, but much of it has come through my own struggles with sin and adversity.

All these factors have both clarified my thinking and helped me to find better ways to explain the process of change in the Christian life. So it seemed a good point to revise *You Can Change*. The overall message and aim are unchanged. I want to show how we can and should approach change in a way that is centred on 'the truth that is in Jesus' (Ephesians 4:21). I want to foreground the work of God, as well as show what it looks like to respond with faith and repentance. Above all, I want to help Christians become more like Jesus in a practical, down-to-earth, easy-to-understand way that is rooted in God's transforming grace.

I've retained the structure of ten chapters shaped around ten questions because this provides a clear route for readers to apply what they're reading to their own lives. But I've made changes to every chapter – adding clarifications, moderating overstatements, anticipating questions. Some changes have been more substantial, introducing new material and involving revising larger sections. At the same time, I didn't want to make the book more daunting to read, so I've also removed material that I no longer thought was helpful or necessary.

Alongside this revised edition of *You Can Change*, I've written a new companion devotional book of daily reflections on Scripture. Its ten chapters follow the same ten questions that are in this book, so the two books can be read in tandem. In my ideal scenario, people will read a chapter of *You Can Change*, meet up once a week to discuss it, and read the devotional book each day at the same time. But neither *You Can Change* nor its devotional companion need to be read alongside each other.

This is my prayer for you as you read this book:

that your love may abound more and more in knowledge and depth of insight, so that you may be able to discern what is best and may be pure and blameless for the day of Christ, filled with the fruit of righteousness that comes through Jesus Christ – to the glory and praise of God.
(Philippians 1:9–11)

Introduction

- Jack started struggling with lust in his teens. Access to porn on the Internet made matters worse. Twenty years or so later, he's still fighting sinful fantasies. He thought marriage would sort it all out, but it didn't. He's put in place regimes of spiritual discipline. All to no avail.
- You'd think Carla was a respectable Christian. She doesn't swear, steal, get drunk, commit adultery or do any of the sins that we use to measure one another's godliness. But her Christian service has little joy. Often she's irritable; often complaining.
- Colin's life was turned round when he converted. He left an adulterous relationship and stopped getting drunk. But, a few years on, his Christian growth seems to have plateaued. Like Carla, he looks respectable enough, but those close to him know that he has a temper. He's not someone you want to cross.
- If shopping were an Olympic sport, Emma would be a medal contender. She's not had an easy life and shopping cheers her up. New clothes, something for the home, luxury foods – these are the bright spots in her life. They're her compensations. But it means that money is tight and she has little to give to others.
- Everyone said that Jamal would be a great asset: he was godly, diligent, taught well. But it soon became apparent that his diligence was driven by a need to prove himself. He 'needed' a role, but his fear of failure was debilitating. There were dark moods with periods of withdrawal.
- Baptising Kate had been the highlight of my year, but where to begin now? With her racism? Her drinking? Her innuendo? She had gladly accepted the call to be ready to die for Christ,

but how would she respond to the call to sobriety? How would that be good news?

Is there hope for these people? I'm convinced there is. There's the hope of change through Jesus. I know there's hope because, though I've created composite pictures and changed details, I *know* Jack, Carla, Colin, Emma, Jamal and Kate.

- When Jack went through an early version of this material with me, he stopped masturbating almost overnight. The struggle with porn has continued, with some lapses but also many victories. Every now and then he sends a text asking for prayer and suggesting that I ask 'the question' next time we see each other.
- Carla has blossomed. There hasn't been a massive change of behaviour, but her attitude is radically different. She often expresses her delight in God and amazement at his grace. She serves willingly, looks for opportunities, takes initiatives. When she speaks of others' faults, it's with grief and love, accompanied by affirmation.
- Colin has a new lease of life, with a growing delight in God. He still has occasions when he feels angry, but he knows his anger reflects a desire for control, so he responds with repentance. He's learning to trust God's care in those moments.
- Emma still likes shopping, but she has other things to do now and other places to turn. She's too busy cooking for others or looking after their children. The highlights of her week are times with other Christians. She's learning to find refuge in God.
- Jamal is a lot more relaxed. It's still a challenge not to let failures overwhelm him, but it's been delightful to see him resting in God's grace. With this has come a freedom to serve, both at work and in the community.
- It's been a joy to see Kate grow as a Christian. Some changes we've had to talk with her about; others have taken place naturally as she's seen more of Christ's glory. It's not always

been straightforward, but gradually Kate is working it out for herself. I can't help smiling when I hear her begin, 'I think maybe I ought to . . . '

Many books are written by experts. This book isn't one of them. It was written out of my own struggle to change. My long battle with particular issues set me searching the Scriptures and writers from the past. This book shares the wonderful truths I discovered that give me hope. For years I wondered if I'd ever overcome certain sins in my life. I can't claim to have conquered sin – no one can in this life – but here are truths that have led to change in my life and the lives of others.

You may be a new Christian, struggling to change the habits of your former way of life. You may be an older Christian who feels like you've plateaued – you grew quickly when you first believed, but now your Christian life is much of a muchness. You may be a Christian who's fallen into sin in a big way and you're wondering how you'll ever get back on track. You may be helping other Christians grow and, while you can tell them about the way they should live, you're not sure how to help them get there.

This book is about *hope*. It's about the hope that we have in Jesus. It's about hope for forgiveness, but also about hope for change. Not that this book alone will change you. We're not changed by systems or rules. We need a Redeemer to set us free and we have a great Redeemer in Jesus. So this book points to Jesus and explains how faith in Jesus leads to change – what theologians call 'sanctification' or becoming more like Jesus.

You can change. Maybe you've kind of given up. Like me, you may have tried many times already. Like me, you may have read books that gave you lots of things to do. Please don't despair. I believe that you can experience *hope for a change*. I've read books full of good theology and I've read books full of day-to-day advice. What this book tries to do is *connect* the truth about God with our Monday-morning struggles.

One of our problems is that we think of holiness as giving up things we enjoy out of a vague sense of obligation. But I'm convinced that holiness is *always, always good news*. God calls us to the good life. He's always bigger and better than anything sin offers. The key is to realise why change is good news in your specific struggles with sin.

So I want to encourage you to work on a particular issue in your life as you read this book – your 'change project'. Each chapter takes the form of a question that you can ask of your change project, with more questions at the end of the chapter to help explore this further. There are reflection sections with exercises and quotes that can be used for individual meditation or group discussion. Let me also encourage you to read with a friend or group, so you can provide encouragement and accountability to one another as you work on your change projects.

So let's begin with our first question . . .

1

What would you like to change?

What would you like to change? Maybe you'd choose to change your appearance or find a partner or work out how to improve your children's behaviour. Would you like to be one more step up the career ladder or maybe to get a foot *on* it? Would you like to be more confident and wittier? Or maybe to be less angry or depressed? Would you like to have more control over your emotions?

We all want to change in some way. Some of these are good things to want; others not so good. The problem with all of them is that they're not ambitious enough! God offers us something more – much, much more.

Created in God's image

In the opening chapter of the Bible, we read that 'God created mankind in his own image, in the image of God he created them' (Genesis 1:26–27). We were made to be God's image on earth – to know him, to share his rule over the world, to reflect his glory. The idea is probably like that of a statue of a god who represents the authority and glory of that god. We're not to make images of the living God because *we* are his image. We're God's representatives on earth. We're God's glory. We display his likeness.

After each day of creation, God declares what he's made to be 'good'. But on the sixth day, God's verdict on a world that now includes humanity is that it is '*very* good' (Genesis 1:31). God's work wasn't finished until there was something in the world to reflect his glory in it. We often excuse our actions, saying, 'I'm only human', but there's nothing 'only' about being human. We're truly human as we reflect God's glory.

A broken image

The problem is that this is now a broken image. That's because humanity rejected God. We try to live our lives our way and we make a mess of things. We struggle to be God's image on earth. We no longer reflect his glory as we should. God's verdict on humanity is this: 'all have sinned and fall short of the glory of God' (Romans 3:23). 'Paul's language here,' comments Sinclair Ferguson, 'is loaded with the biblical motif of the divine image. In Scripture, image and glory are interrelated ideas. As the image of God, man was created to reflect, express and participate in the glory of God, in miniature, creaturely form.'[1] We've failed to be the images of God we were made to be. We can't be the people we *want* to be, let alone the people we *should* be.

A true image

Enter Jesus: 'the image of God' (2 Corinthians 4:4).

> The Son is the image of the invisible God, the firstborn over all creation.
> (Colossians 1:15)

> The Son is the radiance of God's glory and the exact representation of his being.
> (Hebrews 1:3)

> The Word became flesh and made his dwelling among us. We have seen his glory, the glory of the one and only Son, who came from the Father, full of grace and truth.
> (John 1:14)

Jesus is the glory of the Father. He makes God known in the world. He is God in human form. He shows us what it means to be the image of God and to reflect God's glory. That's why the New

---

1 Sinclair B. Ferguson, *The Holy Spirit* (Leicester: IVP, 1996), pp. 139–40.

Testament sometimes says we should be like God and sometimes that we should be like Christ. It's because Christ is the true image of God.

So Jesus shows us God's agenda for change. 'It is Christ who supplies the pattern for the renewal of the new self,' says Douglas Moo.[2]

God isn't interested in making us religious. Think of Jesus. He was hated by religious people. God isn't interested in making us 'spiritual' either, if by spiritual you mean detached. Jesus was God getting stuck in. God isn't interested in making us self-absorbed. Jesus was self-giving personified. God isn't interested in serenity. Jesus was passionate for God, angry at sin and wept over the city. The word 'holy' means 'consecrated'. For Jesus, holiness didn't mean being set apart *from* the world but being consecrated *to* God *in* the world. He was God's glory *in* and *for* the world.

The glory of God is the sum of all that he is: his love, goodness, beauty, purity, judgement, splendour, power, wisdom and majesty. The earthly life of Jesus reflected the glory of God in the goodness of his actions, the beauty of his attitudes and the purity of his thoughts. He reflected the power of God in what appears to us a more topsy-turvy way. He displayed the infinite freedom and grace of God not by clinging to splendour but by voluntarily giving it up in love to rescue us (Philippians 2:6–8). Jesus is the true image of God, displaying God's glory through his life and through his death.

'At least I can put my feet up when I get home,' Colin told himself as he nudged through the traffic. But when he walked through the door, their youngest was screaming and his wife was going on about a broken vacuum cleaner. 'Give us a break,' he muttered, slumping in the chair.

Jamal came back to his desk with a mug of coffee. It was mid-afternoon – the graveyard shift. His hand wavered over the mouse button. He looked at his in tray. Then he clicked on solitaire. Yes, he'd work. But a quick game first.

---

2   D. J. Moo, *The Letters to the Colossians and to Philemon*, Pillar New Testament Commentary (Nottingham: Apollos, 1996), p. 68.

'I'm a grown woman,' Kate told herself. But she loved being in Pete's presence. He seemed to understand her – much better than her husband. Lately, her marriage had seemed hollow. She paused, then took the long route round, past Pete's desk. She didn't want sex or anything. Just a smile.

It had gone on for three years. Three years of patiently teaching and doing good with only misunderstanding and hostility in return. He wanted to say, 'I quit, I don't need this.' But instead he said, 'Not my will, but yours be done.' A few hours later, he hung on a cross. Nails cutting into his limbs. Lungs struggling for air. Crowds spitting venom. He wanted to say, 'I quit, I'm coming down.' But instead he said, 'Father, forgive' (Luke 23:34). He kept going until he could cry, 'It is finished' (John 19:30).

Jesus is the perfect person, the true image of God, the glory of the Father. And God's agenda for change is for us to become like Jesus:

> And we know that in all things God works for the good of those who love him, who have been called according to his purpose. For those God foreknew he also predestined to be conformed to the image of his Son, that he might be the firstborn among many brothers and sisters. And those he pre-destined, he also called; those he called, he also justified; those he justified, he also glorified.
> (Romans 8:28–30)

> Follow God's example, therefore, as dearly loved children and live a life of love, just as Christ loved us and gave himself up for us as a fragrant offering and sacrifice to God.
> (Ephesians 5:1–2; see also 1 Corinthians 11:1; Philippians 2:5; 1 Peter 2:21)

> Whoever claims to live in [God] must live as Jesus did.
> (1 John 2:6; see also 3:16–17; 4:10–11)

In Romans 8, Paul says God uses everything that happens to us to make us like Jesus – both the good things and the bad things.

Indeed, the bad things become in some sense good for us because they make us like Jesus. They may be evil in themselves, but God uses them for the good of those who love him, and that 'good' is our becoming like Jesus.

This isn't a let-down. We shouldn't be disappointed that the promise of good things turns out to be conformity to Christ. It's not like offering a child something good from the shop and then giving them a salad. We know salad is good for us, but we'd rather enjoy some sweets. Jesus isn't just good *for* us, he is goodness itself. He defines 'good'. The secret of gospel change is being convinced that Jesus himself defines the good life and he is the fountain of all joy. Any alternative we might choose would be the let-down.

Making us like Jesus was God's plan from the beginning. God 'predestined', or planned, for us to be like his Son (Romans 8:29). Before God had even made the world, his plan for you and I was to make us like Jesus. And everything that happens to us is part of this plan. One day, his plan will be complete and we will share God's glory, reflecting it back to him so that he is glorified through us (Romans 8:30).

I was dropping my daughter off at school. It was the day of her school Easter service and she was playing Jesus, miming as the class acted out the triumphal entry into Jerusalem. On the way, we picked up Anna – a young Christian girl who'd been baptised in our church a few months before. As Anna was getting out of the car, she shouted to my daughter, 'Be a good Jesus today.' 'Same to you,' I shouted back. Except, of course, I wasn't quick-witted enough to do it until after Anna had shut the car door and walked away.

Be a good Jesus. Our job is to study the glory of God revealed in the life and death of Jesus. We're to study his character, learn his role and understand his motivation so that in every situation we can improvise his part. We'll face situations that Jesus never faced but, if we understand his character well enough, we'll be able to improvise. We'll be a good Jesus.

Recreated in God's image

I'd like to play football like Lionel Messi. I could watch videos of Messi in action. I could study what he does. I might even persuade him to tutor me. All this might even lead to a small improvement in my abilities. But it's not going to turn me into a great footballer.

I want to be like Jesus. I can observe him in action as I read the Gospels. I can study the life he lived and the love he showed. I could try very hard to imitate him. But at best that would only lead to a small, short-lived improvement. Indeed, even that small improvement would probably only make me proud.

The great news is that Jesus is not only my example; he's also my Redeemer.

'If anyone is in Christ,' says 2 Corinthians 5:17, 'the new creation has come; the old has gone, the new is here!' When you become a Christian, something amazing happens: there's a new creation. The power of God that made the sun and stars is focused down like a laser into your heart. God steps into the world, as it were, and creates all over again. We're transformed, reborn, made new. 'For God, who said, "Let light shine out of darkness," made his light shine in our hearts to give us the light of the knowledge of God's glory displayed in the face of Christ' (2 Corinthians 4:6). God spoke a word into the darkness and there was light. He spoke a word into the chaos and there was beauty. And now God again speaks a word through the gospel. He speaks into the darkness of our hearts and there is light. He speaks into the chaos of our lives and there is beauty.

What does it mean for us to be a new creation? It means we're re-created in the image of God. It means we're given new life so we can grow like Christ. And being like Christ means being like God: it means reflecting God's glory as God's image.

> Put on the new self, created to be like God in true righteousness and holiness.
> (Ephesians 4:24)

> Just as we have borne the image of the earthly man, so shall we bear the image of the heavenly man [Jesus].
> (1 Corinthians 15:49)

> Do not lie to each other, since you have taken off your old self with its practices and have put on the new self, which is being renewed in knowledge in the image of its Creator.
> (Colossians 3:9–10)

Jesus came to remake us in God's image. He's the second Adam. Everyone takes their imprint from our common ancestor, the first Adam. We were made in Adam's image. That should have meant we were made in *God*'s image but, in fact, it means we're made in a broken image of him. We all have an in-built bias against God. But Jesus is the second Adam, and all who are united to Jesus by faith are being made new in Christ's image, which is the image of God as it should have been. Jesus took our brokenness, our hatred, our curse, he took all this on himself on the cross. He took the penalty of our sin and gave us in its place a new life and a new love. Charles Wesley put it like this in his famous hymn 'Hark! The herald angels sing':

> Adam's likeness now efface,
> stamp thine image in its place:
> Second Adam from above,
> recreate us in thy love.

'Efface' means 'wipe' or 'rub out'. God is like an artist sketching a portrait of Jesus on to our lives. He takes his eraser and rubs out the ugly features in our lives and carefully draws in the beauty of Jesus.

God is in the business of change. And the change he's interested in is to make us like Jesus. God is restoring his image in us so that we can know him again, rule with him and reflect his glory.

Seeing glory and reflecting glory

> We are not like Moses, who would put a veil over his face to prevent the Israelites from seeing the end of what was passing away. But their minds were made dull, for to this day the same veil remains when the old covenant is read. It has not been removed, because only in Christ is it taken away. Even to this

day when Moses is read, a veil covers their hearts. But whenever anyone turns to the Lord, the veil is taken away. Now the
Lord is the Spirit, and where the Spirit of the Lord is, there
is freedom. And we all, who with unveiled faces contemplate
the Lord's glory, are being transformed into his image with
ever-increasing glory, which comes from the Lord, who is the
Spirit.
(2 Corinthians 3:13–18)

When Moses came down from Mount Sinai after meeting with
God, his face shone with the reflected glory of God. So much
so that the Israelites were terrified and he had to cover his face
(Exodus 34:29–35). Paul says that, in a sense, this veil remains to
the present day. People don't recognise the glory of God because
they don't recognise Christ. So their hearts shrink in fear from
God's glory.

But 'whenever anyone turns to the Lord, the veil is taken away'
(2 Corinthians 3:16). When Moses was in the tabernacle before
God, he could take the veil off because he was turned towards God
and not towards the people (Exodus 34:34). It's the same when we
turn to God in repentance. The veil that hides God's glory is taken
away. Our eyes are opened to see the glory of God in Christ.

Moses coming down the mountain after meeting God was a
picture of what should have been. Moses radiated God's glory
because he saw God's glory. That's how it should have been for all
humanity.

And that's how it can be again. We can be glory reflectors –
people who radiate divine glory. When we turn to Jesus we see
the glory of God. We see, says Paul a few verses later, 'God's glory
displayed in the face of Christ' (2 Corinthians 4:6). And when we
see the glory of God, our lives shine with that glory. It transforms
us so that we reflect God's glory, bringing light to the world and
praise to God. We reflect God's glory when we see God's glory in
the face of Christ.

The message of this book is that change takes place in our lives
when we turn to see the glory of God in Jesus. We 'see' the glory of

Christ as we 'hear' the gospel of Christ (vv. 4–6). Moral effort, fear of judgement, sets of rules can't bring lasting change. But amazing things happen when we turn to the Lord (3:16).

First, 'the Lord is the Spirit, and where the Spirit of the Lord is, there is freedom' (v. 17). On our own, we can't be the people we want to be. We certainly can't be people who reflect God's glory. We're trapped by our emotions and desires. But, when we turn to the Lord, Jesus sets us free through the Holy Spirit. Instead of hearts that shrink in fear from God's glory, we receive hearts that delight in his glory. We're no longer motivated by the fear of law but by the opportunity to experience divine glory.

Second, 'we . . . with unveiled faces contemplate the Lord's glory' (v. 18). When we turn to the Lord, we begin again to display God's glory. We become like Moses, our faces shining with the radiant glory of God.

Third, 'we . . . are being transformed into his image' (v. 18). When we turn to the Lord, we become more like Jesus – people of grace and truth, love and purity.

Fourth, when we turn to the Lord we're changed 'with ever-increasing glory' (v. 18). We're changed 'from one degree of glory to another' (v. 18, ESV). We already reflect God's glory and we reflect his glory more as we increasingly appreciate his glory in Christ. And one day we will be glorified and enjoy him for ever. The time of Moses was glorious (3:7). The present is more glorious (3:8). The future is 'ever-increasing glory' (v. 18). Puritan Thomas Watson said sanctification – this process of change – 'is heaven begun in the soul'. 'Sanctification and glory differ only in degree,' he continued. 'Sanctification is glory in the seed, and glory is sanctification in the flower.'[3]

So who do you want to be like? How would you like to change? Please don't settle for anything less than being like Jesus and reflecting the glory of God. And what must we do if we want to reflect God's glory? Look on the glory of God in the face of Jesus Christ.

---

3 Thomas Watson, *A Body of Divinity* (Edinburgh: Banner of Truth, 1965), p. 242.

Most of us don't live lives considered great by the world. For us, holiness consists not in heroic acts but a thousand small decisions. But God gives us the opportunity to fill the mundane and the ordinary with his glory. We can be radiators of divine glory in a drab world; reflectors of his light in a dark world. Here's Charles Wesley again:[4]

> Finish then, thy new creation,
> pure and spotless let us be;
> let us see thy great salvation
> perfectly restored in thee:
> changed from glory into glory,
> till in heaven we take our place;
> till we cast our crowns before thee,
> lost in wonder, love and praise!

Reflection #1

Think of specific people you consider to be Christlike in good measure. What is it about them that makes them like Jesus? What is it about them that's attractive? What has happened in their life to make them the people they are? What do they think about themselves? What do they think about Jesus?

Reflection #2

'Whoever wants to be my disciple must deny themselves and take up their cross and follow me' (Mark 8:34). The service, submission and suffering seen in the cross are the special marks of what it means to be like Jesus. How does the New Testament apply this to our attitude to:

- other Christians (see Romans 15:7 and Philippians 2:1–11)
- cultural influences and peer pressure (see Galatians 6:14)

---

4   Charles Wesley, 'Love divine, all loves excelling', 1747.

- those in need (see 2 Corinthians 8:8–9 and 1 John 3:16)
- our partner or spouse (see Ephesians 5:22–33)
- suffering (see 1 Peter 2:19–25)
- sin (see 1 Peter 4:1–2)?

Change project

Question 1: What would you like to change?

Think of an area of your life that you'd like to change. It might be a behaviour (lying, lust, overeating, excessive spending or inappropriate relationships) or it might be an emotion (depression, envy, anxiety, greed or anger). It might be a Christian virtue or a fruit of the Spirit that you feel is particularly lacking in your life.

Is your change project about changing your behaviour or emotions?

It's no good choosing a change you would like to see in someone else. You can't choose 'well-behaved children' or 'more attentive friends'. You must choose something about *you* – such as 'not shouting at my children' or 'getting less irritated by my housemates'.

Is your change project about something specific?

Try not to choose something too general – 'be a better parent', for example. Choose a specific behaviour or emotion. It should be specific enough that you can remember the last time you did it or felt it.

What would it mean for you to be more like Jesus?

- You may have thought about the *negative* behaviour and emotions you would like to change. What's the positive?
- Describe the goal of your change project.
- How would Jesus behave or think in your situation?
- Can you think of any stories or teaching of Jesus that illustrate what you should be like?

Write a summary of what you would like to change.

2

Why would you like to change?

Why would you like to change? Think about it for a moment. Why do you want to be more like Jesus? Why do you want to keep a lid on your temper or overcome lust or stop living in a fantasy world? Why do you want to feel less depressed or bitter or frustrated? Why do you want to be a better parent, a better spouse, a better friend, a better employee? Here are three answers you may have given.

1 To prove ourselves to God

You may want to change so God will be impressed with you, bless you in some way or save you.

Many people think good people go to heaven. So if you want to go to heaven, you need to be good. We kind of think of heaven as a fancy nightclub with a bouncer on the door. The bouncer only lets in smartly dressed people. Anyone in jeans or trainers is turned away. So we have to smarten ourselves up to get into heaven.

Or you may think you'll be accepted on the last day because of God's grace, but you still feel the need to impress God so he'll bless you in the meantime. 'I've tried living God's way,' one woman told me, 'but he still hasn't given me a husband.' She wanted to impress God so he'd give her what she wanted.

The instinct to self-atone runs deep in our hearts. We want to make amends for our sin on our own. But God has done it all through Christ because of his grace, his love given to us even though it is undeserved. Grace is so simple to understand, yet so hard to grasp. The problem is that we seem to be hardwired to think we must do something to make God favourably disposed towards us. We want to take the credit. All the time God is saying, 'In my love I gave my Son for you. He's done everything needed to secure my blessing. I love you as you are and I accept you in him.' God can't love you more than he does now – no matter how much you change your life. And God won't love you less than he does now – no matter what mess you make of your life. 'God demonstrates his own love for us in this: *while we were still sinners*, Christ died for us' (Romans 5:6–9).

2 To prove ourselves to other people

This is often the reason I want to change: I want people to be impressed by me. We may want to fit in or win approval. We certainly don't want people finding out what we're like inside. We wear masks to hide our real selves. Wearing the mask can be a great strain – it's like acting a role all the time – but we dare not let people see us as we really are.

One of the problems with trying to prove ourselves to other people is that they set the standard. Their standards may be ungodly but we adopt their behaviour to fit in. Their standards may be godly but we're living in obedience to people rather than in obedience to God. Often what happens is we settle for living like other people even when that falls short of living like Jesus. Or we measure ourselves against other people and decide we're more righteous. We may point the finger at others' faults so we can feel better about ourselves.

Instead, we should be comparing ourselves to Jesus. Then, we will find that we fall a long way short of God's standards and discover we desperately need a saviour.

3 To prove ourselves to ourselves

Another common reason why we want to change is so we can feel good about ourselves. When we mess up, we feel the shame of our sin, so we want to put things right. We want to think of ourselves as 'a *former* user of porn' rather than a 'porn addict'. We want to say 'I *used* to have a problem with anger' rather than 'I have a problem with anger'. So when we mess up, our primary concern is that we can't think of ourselves as 'a *former* sinner'. We can't feel good about ourselves until we've a put some distance between us and our last 'big sin'. For us, sin has become first and foremost sin against ourselves. If I sin, then I've let myself down. What I feel when I sin is the offence against me and my self-esteem, not the offence against God.

Justified by grace

What's wrong with wanting to change so we can prove ourselves to God, other people or ourselves? One answer is that it doesn't work. We might fool other people for a while. We might even fool ourselves. But we can never change enough to impress God. And here's the reason. Trying to impress God, others or ourselves puts *us* at the centre of our change project. It makes change all about *me* looking good. It's done for *my* glory – and that's pretty much the definition of sin. Sin is living for my glory instead of God's. Sin is living my way for me instead of living God's way for God. Often that means rejecting God as Lord and wanting to be our own lord, but it can also involve rejecting God as Saviour and wanting to be our own saviour. Pharisees do good works and repent their bad works. But gospel repentance includes repenting good works done for the wrong reasons. We repent trying to be our own saviour. Theologian John Gerstner says, 'The thing that really separates us from God is not so much our sin, but our damnable good works.'[1] George Whitefield, a great eighteenth-century evangelist, put it like this:

> Before you can speak peace in your heart, you must not only be made sick of your original and actual sin, but you must be made sick of your righteousness, of all your duties and performances. There must be a deep conviction before you can be brought out of your self-righteousness; it is the last idol taken out of our heart. The pride of our heart will not let us submit to the righteousness of Jesus Christ. But . . . if you never felt

---

1 Cited in Timothy Keller, 'Preaching to the heart', audio lectures (Ockenga Institute, Gordon-Conwell Theological Seminary, 2006), available at: www.gordonconwell.edu/tim-keller-resources.

the deficiency of your own righteousness, you cannot come to Jesus Christ.[2]

Deep down in all of us, there's a tendency to want to prove ourselves; to base our worth on what we do. Religious people do this, but so do most non-religious people. They do a secular version in which their identity is based on their performance. I feel good about myself because I'm a success at work or because I dress to impress or because I'm great in bed.

As Christians, too, we continually slip back into trying to be our own saviour. At the end of the Sermon on the Mount, Jesus presents us with two choices, two roads, two foundations for life (Matthew 7:13–27). We might suppose the choice is between a good life and a bad life. But when you look back over the sermon, that's not what you see. The alternative life that Jesus rejects is a good life lived for the wrong reasons. He rejects the 'righteousness . . . of the Pharisees' (5:20). They think they're righteous for God, but really they're doing it for themselves (7:21–23) – 'to be honoured by others' or to manipulate God (6:1–8). Their righteousness doesn't come from the heart (5:21–48). So the options Jesus presents are self-righteousness and poverty of spirit (5:3).

Another word we use when 'proving' ourselves is 'justify'. We want to justify ourselves – to demonstrate that we're worthy of God or respectable to other people. But we're justified through faith in what Christ has done. When you feel the desire to prove yourself, remember that you're already right with God in Christ. You can't do anything to make yourself more acceptable to God than you already are. You don't need to worry whether people are impressed by you because you're justified or vindicated by God. What makes you feel good is not what *you've* done but what *Christ* has done *for you*. Your identity isn't dependent on your change. You're a child of the heavenly King.

---

2 George Whitefield, 'The method of grace', in *Select Sermons of George Whitefield* (Edinburgh: Banner of Truth, 1958), p. 83.

To some who were confident of their own righteousness and looked down on everyone else, Jesus told this parable: 'Two men went up to the temple to pray, one a Pharisee and the other a tax collector. The Pharisee stood by himself and prayed: "God, I thank you that I am not like other people – robbers, evildoers, adulterers – or even like this tax collector. I fast twice a week and give a tenth of all I get."

'But the tax collector stood at a distance. He would not even look up to heaven, but beat his breast and said, "God, have mercy on me, a sinner."

'I tell you that this man, rather than the other, went home justified before God. For all those who exalt themselves will be humbled, and those who humble themselves will be exalted.' (Luke 18:9–14)

The Pharisee wants to impress God. That's why he lists his achievements. And he wants to impress other people. That's why he stands up in a prominent place (Matthew 6:5). No doubt he was pretty impressed with himself. He certainly judges himself as better than the tax collector.

However, the tax collector doesn't think that he's impressive. He stands at a distance from other people. He doesn't claim to be good in any way. He can only cry out to God for mercy. But, says Jesus, it's the tax collector who goes home 'justified'. The Pharisee tries to justify himself but he's not justified. The tax collector relies only on God's mercy, and he is justified.

I remember telling a man that his alcoholic daughter was getting baptised. He was shocked and even a little angry. He had always thought of himself as someone who was good enough for God. In fact, his life was a mess in all sorts of ways, but he maintained the illusion that he was OK with God by pointing out other people's faults. At least he could think of himself as better than them. But, suddenly, here was his alcoholic daughter entering the kingdom of God. She wasn't good enough for God, but that didn't seem to matter. His basis for acceptance by God was suddenly turned upside down.

This brings us to the real problem with changing to impress. God has given his Son for us so that we can be justified. Jesus died on the cross, separated from his Father, bearing the full weight of God's wrath so that we can be accepted by God. When we try to prove ourselves by our good works, we're saying, in effect, that the cross wasn't enough.

Imagine you owe a huge debt that's left you languishing in poverty. Then a relative pays off your creditors. They've given everything that was needed at great cost to themselves. Then you try to give them some loose change as repayment. You let everyone know that you helped repay the debt, it was a joint effort. To do this would be pointless and insulting.

We don't do good works so that we can be saved; we're saved so we can do good works: 'For it is by grace you have been saved, through faith . . . not by works . . . For we are God's handiwork, created in Christ Jesus to do good works, which God prepared in advance for us to do' (Ephesians 2:8–10). The order is clear: salvation comes first and is followed by good works. But many people get this the wrong way round and act as though good works must come first. Because they get this wrong, many non-believers never enjoy salvation. But it's also true that, because many Christians don't fully grasp the order of salvation and good works, they don't enjoy the good works of holiness. Dane Ortlund says,

> There are two ways to live the Christian life. You can live it either *for* the heart of Christ or *from* the heart of Christ. You can live for the smile of God or from it. For a new identity as a son or daughter of God or from it. For your union with Christ or from it.[3]

You will cleanse no sin from your life that you have not first recognised to be pardoned through the cross. This is because holiness always starts in the heart. The essence of holiness is not new

---

3 Dane C. Ortlund, *Gentle and Lowly: The heart of Christ for sinners and sufferers* (Wheaton, IL: Crossway, 2020), p. 181.

behaviour, new activity or new disciplines. Holiness is new affections, new desires, new motives that then lead to new behaviour. If you don't see your sin as completely pardoned, then your affections, desires and motives will be wrong. Your aim will be to prove yourself. Or your focus will be on the consequences of your sin rather than hating the sin itself and desiring God in its place.

Sometimes people change their behaviour, but their motives and desires are still wrong, so their new behaviour is no more pleasing to God than their old behaviour. Consider an alcoholic who gives up drink because they fear social stigma or want to save their relationship or don't want to end up in the gutter. It's good that they've given up drink, but they aren't any holier in God's sight because they're still motivated by desires that leave God out of the picture. Or consider a Christian who goes to a prayer meeting to impress people or feel good about themselves or avoid a friend's rebuke. Their behaviour has changed, but their motives and desires are unchanged. This isn't holiness – though it may be that praying with other Christians contributes to a change of affections. John Piper says, 'Conversion is the creation of new desires, not just new duties; new delights, not just new deeds; new treasures, not just new tasks.'[4]

This point is illustrated by a story attributed to great nineteenth-century preacher Charles Spurgeon. A humble gardener presents a bunch of carrots to his king because he so esteems and loves his sovereign.[5] The king rewards this love with a plot of land so the gardener can continue to bless the kingdom. A courtier sees this and thinks, 'An acre of land for a bunch of carrots – what a deal!' So the next day the courtier presents the king with a magnificent horse. The wise king, discerning the courtier's heart, simply accepts the gift with a 'thank you'. When the courtier is disconsolate, the king explains. 'The gardener gave the carrots to me, but you have given the horse to yourself. You gave not for love of me, but love

---

4   John Piper, *When I Don't Desire God: How to fight for God* (Wheaton, IL: Crossway, 2004), p. 16.

5   Cited in Timothy Keller, *The Prodigal God: Recovering the heart of the Christian faith* (London: Hodder & Stoughton, 2008), pp. 60–2.

of yourself in the hope of a reward.' The question Spurgeon leaves us with is, are you feeding the hungry or are you feeding yourself? Are you clothing the naked or are you seeking your own reward? Are you serving God or serving yourself? The Bible talks often of reward, but that reward is God himself – the joy of knowing and pleasing the God we love and in whom we delight.

So we don't change to prove ourselves to God. We're accepted by God so that we can change. God gives us a new identity and this new identity is the motive and basis for change.

A new identity

Again and again in the New Testament we're called to 'be what we are'. It's not about achieving something so you can impress; it's about living out the new identity that God gives us in Jesus.

> His divine power has given us everything we need for a godly life through our knowledge of him who called us by his own glory and goodness. Through these he has given us his very great and precious promises, so that through them you may participate in the divine nature, having escaped the corruption in the world caused by evil desires.
>
> For this very reason, make every effort to add to your faith goodness; and to goodness, knowledge; and to knowledge, self-control; and to self-control, perseverance; and to perseverance, godliness; and to godliness, mutual affection; and to mutual affection, love. For if you possess these qualities in increasing measure, they will keep you from being ineffective and unproductive in your knowledge of our Lord Jesus Christ. But whoever does not have them is short-sighted and blind, forgetting that they have been cleansed from their past sins.
> (2 Peter 1:3–9)

We don't need anything new to be godly because we already have all we need. The great and precious promises that shape our new identity enable us to be like God. Growth in godliness begins with faith in those promises. Notice the problem when someone is ineffective and unproductive. People are 'forgetting that they have been cleansed from their past sins' (v. 9b). They've lost sight of their new identity.

Let's look at three ways the Bible talks about our new identity and see how they provide us with strong motives for change.

1 You are a child of the Father

> When the set time had fully come, God sent his Son, born of a woman, born under the law, to redeem those under the law, that we might receive adoption to sonship. Because you are his sons, God sent the Spirit of his Son into our hearts, the Spirit who calls out, 'Abba, Father.' So you are no longer a slave, but God's child; and since you are his child, God has made you also an heir . . . You, my brothers and sisters, were called to be free. But do not use your freedom to indulge the flesh; rather, serve one another humbly in love.
>
> (Galatians 4:4–7; 5:13; see also Romans 6:15–23)

We used to be slaves to sin. We all know this if we stop to think about it. Think about the times you've tried to change but failed. Think about how you don't live up to your own standards. Think about those new year's resolutions that only lasted into the second week of January. We can't be the people we want to be, let alone people who are like Jesus. We were also slaves to the law. Paul is talking about the law of Moses, but what he says is true of any attempt to change using a set of rules. Instead of setting us free, law crushes us. The best it can do is show us how far we are from being the people we should be. It makes us terrified of stepping out of line.

But God sent his Son to buy our freedom. We're no longer slaves with a slave master. Now we're children with a Father. We don't have to worry about proving ourselves because God says, 'You're my child.' We don't have a spirit of fear but a Spirit who prompts us to cry, 'Abba, Father'. We don't have to worry about the future because God has made us his heirs, so all his resources are ours: 'The adoption to sons – that is the foundation of sanctification, the *only* foundation . . . In his faith each has all the possession he requires and can therefore freely and lovingly devote his entire life to the service of his fellow man.'[6]

We were slaves of sin and now we are children of God. It would be crazy to go on living as slaves rather than as God's children. Freedom doesn't mean that we can sin. That's not freedom. That's going back into slavery. Imagine an alcoholic whose addiction has wrecked their life. Someone kindly puts them through rehab and, after several months, they leave, free from addiction. They're not going to say, 'I'm free at last so I'm going to get drunk.' That's not freedom. That's returning to their old slavery. St Augustine says, 'This forgiveness is not a license to commit sin, but a release from sin; that it is a remission of sin, not a permission to sin.'[7] Our sanctification is not a price we pay or a debt that we owe in return for our forgiveness. Sanctification is a wonderful gift! God has set us free from the penalty and power of sin so that we might *be free* from sin's pollution and pain.

It was Sophie's first day with her adoptive parents. She stalked nervously round her new home, fearing one of the beatings she used to get if something was broken. The toys in her room went untouched – she couldn't quite believe that they were hers. At dinner, she secretly stuffed food in her pocket (you never knew where your next meal would come from when you were on the streets). That night, she felt so alone in her big room. She would have cried if she hadn't long since learned to suppress emotion.

Now listen to her new mother one year on: 'She crawled into bed with me last night, because she was having a bad dream. She curled up next to me, put her head on my chest, told me that she loved me, smiled, and went to sleep. I nearly cried with contentment.'

Sophie had a new identity on day one: she'd become a child in a new family. But, initially, she still lived like a child of the street. Her

---

6   G. C. Berkouwer, *Faith and Sanctification* (Grand Rapids, MI: Eerdmans, 1952), p. 33.

7   St Augustine, *On Faith and Works*, trans. Gregory J. Lombardo (New York: The Newman Press, 1988), XX.36, p. 44.

actions and attitudes were shaped by her old identity. Christians, too, have a new identity, and we're to live out our new identity; to be what we are. So don't live like a slave when you can live like a child of the King of heaven.

2 You are the bride of the Son

> Husbands, love your wives, just as Christ loved the church and gave himself up for her to make her holy, cleansing her by the washing with water through the word, and to present her to himself as a radiant church, without stain or wrinkle or any other blemish, but holy and blameless.
> (Ephesians 5:25–27)

The Church is the bride of Christ. He has loved us, wooed us, cleansed us, rescued us and won us. Our relationship with Christ is a relationship of love and intimacy. It is a union – an exclusive union.

Why do I bring my wife a cup of tea in bed in the morning? It's not because I need to make her mine. She's already my wife, just as Christ is already my bridegroom. It's not because I need to make sure that she doesn't leave me. She's committed herself to me with the covenant promises of marriage, just as Christ has committed himself to me with covenant promises. It's not even so that she'll treat me well. She often treats me well even when I treat her badly, just as Christ is always gracious towards me. No, I try to please my wife because I love her and because she loves me. I delight in delighting her. So it is with Christ. Christ is our lover, our partner, our bridegroom, and so we live for him, we want to please him, we want to do what he asks. The more my wife loves me, the more I find myself loving her. Christ has loved me with infinite love, giving himself for me on the cross. He loved me when I was unlovely. If I'm holy, clean or radiant, it's only because he made me so. And so I love him and live for him.

The Bible often describes sin as 'adultery' (Jeremiah 3:7–8; 5:7; Ezekiel 23:37; Matthew 12:39; James 4:4; Revelation 2:22). Sin is like adultery because it's a betrayal of our true and best love. Why would you do that? The 'love' of an adulterous lover is no love at all. Sin doesn't love us. It tries to use us, abuse us, enslave us, control us and, ultimately, destroy us. Sin takes from us and gives nothing in return. It may use enticing and seductive lies. It may promise the world. But it's all lies. Sin never brings true and lasting satisfaction. Why would you leave a husband as good, loving, gracious, strong, able and beautiful as Jesus for some cheap alternative?

This is how Paul put it to the Christians in Corinth:

> I am jealous for you with a godly jealousy. I promised you to one husband, to Christ, so that I might present you as a pure virgin to him. But I am afraid that just as Eve was deceived by the serpent's cunning, your minds may somehow be led astray from your sincere and pure devotion to Christ.
> (2 Corinthians 11:2–3)

One woman put it to me like this: 'As a child I dreamed of my wedding day, of walking down the aisle in a beautiful white dress. In none of my dreams was my dress covered in dirt and grime.'

We're to live out our new identity, to be what we are. And that means being a pure, devoted, loving bride of Christ.

3 You are the home of the Holy Spirit

> Flee from sexual immorality. All other sins a person commits are outside the body, but whoever sins sexually, sins against their own body. Do you not know that your bodies are temples of the Holy Spirit, who is in you, whom you have received from God? You are not your own; you were bought at a price. Therefore honour God with your bodies.
> (1 Corinthians 6:18–20)

The Temple in the Old Testament was a holy place. Nothing impure was allowed. Now we ourselves are the holy place of God. Our lives and our life together as a Christian community are sacred spaces, consecrated to God.

Christians have come to use the term 'sanctification' to describe the lifetime process of being changed into Christ's likeness. But when the New Testament talks about Christians being 'sanctified', it usually refers to a past, definitive action by God.[8] We have been consecrated by God for his service and made new by the Holy Spirit. Our role is to live out this new identity as God's 'holy ones' or 'saints'.

Imagine you've done the cleaning at home because you have guests coming. You've scrubbed the floors, cleaned the windows, tidied the rooms, dusted the furniture. Everything is spick and span. Then you pop out to get some flowers from the shops through rain and mud. What do you do when you get back? Do you tramp your muddy feet through the house and shake out your wet clothes everywhere? No, you carefully take everything off at the door. You want to keep your home clean for your guests. The Holy Spirit has cleansed us and washed us. He's given us a new start and a new life. He's come to make his home in us. He's consecrated our lives as his temple. Why would you want to mess that up by bringing in your dirty habits or returning to your filthy sins? Would you want a friend to live in a tip?

We're to live out our new identity, to be what we are. And that means being a holy temple for God's Spirit.

The challenge for us is to let this new identity define us on Monday mornings. It's easy to sing about being a child of God or the bride of Christ on a Sunday. The challenge is to think of ourselves as a child of God in the classroom on a Monday morning when our classmates jeer at the way we live. The challenge is to think of ourselves as the bride of Christ in the workplace when the banter is coarse and the ambitions are worldly. The challenge is to think of ourselves as the home of the Holy Spirit in the supermarket when everything feels mundane and dreary.

---

8 David Peterson, *Possessed by God: A New Testament theology of sanctification and holiness* (Leicester: Apollos, 1995).

In this life, our actions always carry a faint taint of sin and self. We do what is right because we love God, but also because we want to impress. But the good news is that God always sees our actions through the prism of Christ. They rise up before him scented, as it were, with the sweet perfume of Christ's righteousness. This means that we can and do please God. Again and again, the New Testament encourages us to behave in a way that will please God.[9] We can and do bring God pleasure.

Union and communion

Can you improve your relationship with God by being holy? The answer is not straightforward.[10]

When we want to stress God's grace to us in Christ, we often answer, 'No, we can't improve our relationship with God.' We can't make God love us any more than he already does. One of the 'tests' we sometimes use to check if a person has grasped the grace of God is to ask whether they think their prayers are more likely to be answered after a good day or after a bad day. The answer, of course, is that we come to God through Christ, so we're as welcome after a bad day as we are after a good day.

The problem is that our experience suggests something different. What we do *does* seem to make a difference to our relationship with God. When I sin, prayer seems harder, church seems a burden and joy in Christ seems remote. Does what I do affect my relationship with God? The answer seems to be 'Yes'.

To help us make sense of this, let's turn to John Owen, a Puritan. Owen makes an important distinction between 'union' and 'communion'. 'Union' is the relationship we have with God through Christ; 'communion' is our lived experience of that relationship. 'Our communion with God,' says Owen, 'consists in his communication of himself to us, with our return to him of that which he

---

9 See, for example, Romans 12:1; 14:17–18; 2 Corinthians 2:15; 5:9; Galatians 6:8; Ephesians 5:10; Philippians 4:18; Colossians 1:10; 3:20; 1 Thessalonians 2:4; 1 Timothy 2:3; 5:4.

10 The section is adapted from Tim Chester, 'You can improve your relationship with God', Desiring God, 18 September 2018, available at: www.desiringgod.org/articles/you-can-improve-your-relationship-with-god See also Tim Chester, *Enjoying God: Experience the power and love of God in everyday life* (Epsom: The Good Book Company, 2018).

requires and accepts, flowing from that union which in Jesus Christ we have with him.'[11]

Union with God is a one-way relationship that all flows from divine grace. Our union with God was initiated by the Father in our election, secured by the Son at Calvary and is applied by the Spirit in regeneration. It is all God from start to finish. This explains why we can't improve our relationship with God. It rests on God's electing love, grace and the finished work of Christ. We can come to God in prayer after a bad day just as readily as we can come to him after a good day because Christians are always secure in Christ.

But our communion with God is a two-way relationship in which our actions make a difference. That is, our lived experience of joy in God is affected by what we do. This explains why our actions make a difference. We can't improve our relationship with God, but we can improve our *experience* of the relationship that our union with God in Christ has created.

This leads to *a great assurance*: whenever we sin and fail, we can always fall back on divine grace. Our union with God is unaffected by our actions, so it forms the great foundation of our lives. But the prospect of communion with God also provides us with *a great incentive*: if we respond to the circumstances of our lives with faith, if we resist the lies of temptation, if we make use of the means of grace, then we will have greater joy in Christ – our communion with God will improve. Our sanctification neither *creates* nor *maintains* our relationship with God, but it may *confirm* our relationship with God and *deepen* our experience of it.

Freedom and love

Let's sum up our motive for change. The reason Christians should want to change is *to enjoy the freedom from sin and delight in God that God gives to us through Jesus.* I want to highlight four things from this definition.

---

11 John Owen, *The Works of John Owen*, ed. William H. Goold (Edinburgh: Banner of Truth, 1965), Vol. 2, pp. 8–9, modernised.

First, growing in holiness is not a sad, dutiful drudge. It's about joy. It's discovering true joy – the joy of knowing and serving God. There is self-denial – sometimes hard and painful self-denial – but true self-denial leads to gaining your life. There will be times when we act out of duty, but we do this believing that duty leads to joy, as denying yourself leads to gaining your life (Mark 8:34–38).[12] How often have you reluctantly dragged yourself out on a cold night to pray with others only to find yourself energised and blessed?

Second, change is about living in freedom. We refuse to go back to the chains and filth of our sin. We live in the wonderful freedom that God's given us. We're free to be the people we should be.

Third, change is about discovering the delight of knowing and serving God. Our job is to stop grubbing around in the dirt and, instead, to enjoy knowing God. We give up our cheap imitations and enjoy the real thing. All too often we think of holiness as giving up the pleasures of sin for some worthy, but drab life. But holiness is recognising that the pleasures of sin are empty and temporary, while what God is inviting us to are magnificent, true, full and rich pleasures that last for ever. Holiness is its own reward. Or, better still, God is his own reward. Enjoying God is the motive for obeying God. Puritan William Gurnall writes, 'There are three things considered in the nature of a holy, righteous life that are enough to demonstrate it to be the only pleasant life. It is a life from God; it is a life with God; it is the very life of God.'[13]

Fourth, becoming like Jesus is something that God gives to us. It's not an achievement that we offer to God. It's enjoying the new identity that he has given us in Christ. It begins with his work for us. He has set us free from sin and offers a relationship with himself. Sanctification is the gift of an enabled will. It is not so much a task that we must perform as an ability we're given to live

---

12 On duty and joy, see John Piper, *When I Don't Desire God: How to fight for God* (Wheaton, IL: Crossway, 2004), pp. 219–22.

13 William Gurnall, *The Christian in Complete Armour* (London: Thomas Tegg, 1845), pp. 329–30.

a glorious new life. Justification counters our condemnation by acquitting us; sanctification counters our deadness by giving us life – a life to be lived in holiness in the same way that a child enjoys playing with a delightful present.

It's as though there are two feasts: the feast of God and the feast of sin. We're invited to both. God invites us to find satisfaction in him while temptation entices us with its lies to look for satisfaction in sin. So we're double-booked! We're continually having to choose which feast we attend. This is God's invitation to us:

'Come, all you who are thirsty,
   come to the waters;
and you who have no money,
   come, buy and eat!
Come, buy wine and milk
   without money and without cost.
Why spend money on what is not bread,
   and your labour on what does not satisfy?
Listen, listen to me, and eat what is good,
   and you will delight in the richest of fare.'
(Isaiah 55:1–2)

Sin promises so much, but it doesn't satisfy and its price is high. That price is broken lives, broken relationships and broken hopes. Ultimately, 'the wages of sin is death' (Romans 6:23). But God offers us a feast that satisfies. He offers delight for our souls. The motivation for change and holiness is this: God's feast is so much better! And the price tag reads 'No charge'. It's his gift. Whose feast are you going to attend today?

Reflection #1

Take a look at the following passages. I've taken some verses from the Bible and made them say the *opposite* of what they actually say. See if you can turn them back into what they really say. You can check by looking at Romans 5:1–2 and Ephesians 2:8–10.

When we prove ourselves by living a good life, we have peace with God through what we do. It's what we do that gives us access to God's blessing and a good standing in people's eyes. Doing this enables us to worry less about whether we'll share God's glory.

It's by changing that your problems will be sorted out, through working hard. It's up to us. This is what we can do for God. We're saved by what we do, so we can prove ourselves. If we do the good works that God plans for us, then we can become God's masterpiece, new people in Christ Jesus.

Reflection #2

- Sin promises fun and excitement, but it delivers pain and tragedy.
- Sin promises freedom, but it delivers slavery and addiction.
- Sin promises life and fulfilment, but it delivers emptiness, frustration and death.
- Sin promises gain, but it delivers loss.
- Sin promises that we can get away with it, but the fact is, we don't.[14]

Identify when sin has made one of these promises in your own experience. What did sin actually deliver?

Change project

Question 2: Why would you like to change?

Do you really want to change?

- Does the thought of becoming like Jesus make you feel sad?
- Do you think your life will become boring, unsatisfying and hard?

---

14 Christopher J. H. Wright, *Life Through God's Word: Psalm 119* (Carlisle: Authentic Media, 2006), p. 60.

- Do you think of giving up sin as an unpleasant duty you must do to win God's approval?

Do you want to change for the wrong reasons?

Do you sometimes think:

- God won't bless me today because I've let him down
- God will answer my prayers today because I've been good
- I need to make it up to God because I've sinned
- I need to change so God will accept me on the final day?

If your answer to any of these is 'Yes', then you may be trying to change to impress God.

Do you sometimes:

- ensure that people know about the good things you're doing
- tell 'little white lies' to cover up your failings
- imagine people being impressed because you're so spiritual
- feel like you've let yourself down when you sin?

If you answered 'Yes' to any of these, then you may be trying to change to impress people or feel good about yourself.

What do you think will happen if your change project is successful?

What difference will it make to:

- God's love for you
- people's opinion of you
- how you view yourself?

What can you do to strengthen your desire to change?

If you suspect that you don't really want to change, think what you could do to strengthen your resolve. If you suspect that you may want to change for the wrong reasons (to impress God, to impress people or to feel good about yourself), then think about what you could do to focus on your new identity in Christ. Here are some ideas.

- Compare slavery to sin with being a child of God. Compare adultery with being the bride of Christ. Compare the filth of sin with being a clean home for the Holy Spirit.
- Memorise Romans 5:1–2, Ephesians 2:8–10 or Titus 3:5–8. Use these verses to speak to your heart when you think in these ways.
- On the cross Jesus cried out, 'It is finished' (John 19:30). Imagine yourself answering back, 'Not quite. I need to finish the job. I still need to win God's blessing.' Think how ridiculous and insulting that would be.
- Imagine two homes side by side. In one, God is hosting his feast. In the other, sin is hosting its feast. Compare the two feasts. What satisfaction do they offer? How lasting and real is that satisfaction? What price must you pay for it?

Write a summary of why you want to change, putting it in a way that resonates for you. Add some ideas for how you could strengthen your desire to change.

3

How are you going to change?

'Please forgive me and set me free.' I don't know how many times I've prayed this prayer. It's in the hundreds. 'Father, here I am again, confessing the *same* sin to you.' Every time, I have to remind myself of God's merciful character and gospel promises. I am forgiven. But I also want to change.

Have you despaired of ever changing? Do you think that you're a lost cause? Maybe you think it's different for you. Other people can change, but your history or temptations or problems make it different for you?

The glorious good news of Jesus is that you and I can change.

Part of the problem is that we often try to change in the wrong way.

Trying to change ourselves

Frustrated by my lust, I wrote out a vow. This was it. Never again. I noted the date and imagined looking back in months to come with satisfaction that my struggle had been relegated to history. But it didn't last long. It didn't work. It couldn't work, as I would have realised if I'd paid attention to Colossians 2:20–23:

> Since you died with Christ to the elemental spiritual forces of this world, why, as though you still belonged to the world, do you submit to its rules: 'Do not handle! Do not taste! Do not touch!'? These rules, which have to do with things that are all destined to perish with use, are based on merely human commands and teachings. Such regulations indeed have an appearance of wisdom, with their self-imposed worship, their false humility and their harsh treatment of

the body, but they lack any value in restraining sensual indulgence.

Maybe you think that making a vow or other disciplines are very spiritual. I certainly thought so at the time. But Paul says these have only the 'appearance of wisdom' (v. 23). In reality, they lack 'any value in restraining sensual indulgence' (v. 23). Wasn't that the truth! Sadly, I had to learn that lesson the hard way. Puritan John Flavel said, 'We are more able to stop the sun in its course or make rivers run uphill as by our own skill and power to rule and order our hearts.'[1]

It seems that our first instinct when we want to change is to *do* something. We think such activity will change us. We want a list of dos and don'ts. In Jesus' day, people thought they could be pure through ceremonial washing. Today, it can be spiritual disciplines or sets of laws. I've tried these approaches. I've written out little rituals to do every morning. I've tried to regulate my behaviour with lists. Many of these things are good in themselves. Indeed, we'll discover the role they can play in helping us to grow in holiness in Chapter 8. But our rituals and disciplines can't change us.

> 'Are you so dull?' [Jesus] asked. 'Don't you see that nothing that enters a person from the outside can defile them? . . . What comes out of a person is what defiles them. For it is from within, out of a person's heart, that evil thoughts come – sexual immorality, theft, murder, adultery, greed, malice, deceit, lewdness, envy, slander, arrogance and folly. All these evils come from inside and defile a person.'
> (Mark 7:18–23)

External activities can't change us, says Jesus, because sin comes from within, from our hearts. Our rituals might change our

---

1 Adapted from John Flavel, *Keeping the Heart* (Fearn, Ross-shire: Christian Heritage, 1999), p. 9.

behaviour for a while, but they can't change our hearts. So they can't bring true and lasting holiness. We need heart change.[2]

What law can and can't do

In the early church, many people advocated living by the law of Moses. We become Christians by faith, they said, but we keep going by following the law. At first sight, it looks like a good option. After all, this list is God-given. It produces people who look very serious about their faith. But Paul would have none of it. We continue as we began, he said, through faith in what Jesus has done for us.

> So then, just as you received Christ Jesus as Lord, continue to live your lives in him, rooted and built up in him, strengthened in the faith as you were taught, and overflowing with thankfulness.
> (Colossians 2:6–7)

> You foolish Galatians! Who has bewitched you? Before your very eyes Jesus Christ was clearly portrayed as crucified. I would like to learn just one thing from you: did you receive the Spirit by the works of the law, or by believing what you heard? Are you so foolish? After beginning by means of the Spirit, are you now trying to finish by means of the flesh?
> (Galatians 3:1–3)

Our Christian lives began when we received the Spirit by believing Christ crucified, not when we finally managed to observe the law. It's foolish to think that we can now take over and finish the job through human effort alone. Imagine being carried across Niagara Falls by a skilled tightrope walker. Halfway across you have a choice. You can let them carry you the rest of the way or you can tell them that you think it would be better if you walked the rest of the way under your own steam. We become Christians by faith in

---

2   Richard F. Lovelace, *Dynamics of Spiritual Life: An Evangelical theology of renewal* (Downers Grove, IL: IVP Academic, 1979), pp. 88–91.

Jesus, we stay Christians by faith in Jesus and we grow as Christians by faith in Jesus. Bishop J. C. Ryle writes:

> If we would be sanctified, our course is clear and plain – *we must begin with Christ*. We must go to Him as sinners, with no plea but that of utter need, and cast our souls on Him by faith ... If we would grow in holiness and become more sanctified, we must *continually go on as we began*, and be ever making fresh applications to Christ.[3]

It's not just that trying to live by laws and disciplines is useless, it's a backwards step. It's a step back into slavery, which ends up undermining grace and hope (Galatians 4:8–11; 5:1–5).

What the law *does* do is show us that we can't change ourselves or make ourselves good enough for God. The purpose of the law is to point to the righteousness that Jesus offers (Romans 3:21–22). The law isn't meant to be the starting point for change. It's meant to bring us to an end of ourselves and so drive us into the arms of Jesus, who is the true starting point for change.

Repenting righteousness

We all have a strong tendency to want to live by a list of rules – what's called 'legalism'. I was talking to a group of students about lifestyle issues. They kept asking specific questions: 'What car can I buy?', 'What should I do with my savings?', 'How much should I spend on clothes?' They wanted a list or a law. But even if we could create a massive list to cover every eventuality, it wouldn't work. It wouldn't bring heart change.

Legalism is appealing for two reasons. First, it makes holiness manageable. A heart wholly devoted to God is a tough demand, but a list of ten rules I can cope with. That was the motivation of the expert in law who asked Jesus, 'Who is my neighbour?' Luke tells us that 'he wanted to justify himself', to be able to tick the 'love your

---

3 J. C. Ryle, *Holiness: Its nature, hindrances, difficulties and roots* (Cambridge: James Clarke, 1956), p. 32; see also pp. 49–50.

neighbour' box (Luke 10:29). But Jesus' story of the good Samaritan blew his hopes of a manageable system apart (vv. 30–37).

Second, legalism makes holiness an achievement on our part. 'Yes, I was saved by grace,' the legalist says, 'but I'm the godly person I am today because I've kept this code of behaviour or practised these spiritual disciplines.' One of its by-products is comparison with other people. We check whether we're holier than other people or look down on those who don't appear as good as us.

No one thinks that they're a legalist. They just think of themselves as someone who takes holiness seriously. After all, it has the 'appearance of wisdom' (Colossians 2:20–23). But if you want to see a legalist, take a look in the mirror. Deep in the heart of each one of us is the proud desire to prove ourselves. Sin is wanting to live our lives *our own way without God*. The terrible irony is that we even want to overcome sin our own way *with* God. The struggle against legalism was not done and dusted around 2,000 years ago in Galatia or 500 years ago at the Reformation. The battle with legalism takes place in our hearts every day.

This means that we need to repent not only our sin but also our 'righteousness', which is when we think of it as *our* righteousness that *we* do to prove *ourselves* and think this makes *us* better than other people.

If someone else thinks they have reasons to put confidence in the flesh, I have more: circumcised on the eighth day, of the people of Israel, of the tribe of Benjamin, a Hebrew of Hebrews; in regard to the law, a Pharisee; as for zeal, persecuting the church; as for legalistic righteousness based on the law, faultless.

But whatever were gains to me I now consider loss for the sake of Christ. What is more, I consider everything a loss because of the surpassing worth of knowing Christ Jesus my Lord, for whose sake I have lost all things. I consider them garbage, that I may gain Christ and be found in him, not having a righteousness of my own that comes from the law,

but that which is through faith in Christ – the righteousness that comes from God on the basis of faith.
(Philippians 3:4–9)

Paul's claims to righteousness were impressive. He had more reason than most to have confidence in his achievements. When it came to keeping lists, he was 'faultless'. Yet when he saw Christ, he realised that all his assets were actually liabilities. Everything he had previously considered to be on the profit side of his balance sheet had to be counted as a loss. He discovered that rules-based righteousness is not really righteousness at all. He had to repent 'a righteousness of my own that comes from the law' so that in its place he could receive 'the righteousness that comes from God and is by faith' (v. 9).

Songwriter Bob Kauflin describes a three-year period of hopelessness in his life characterised by depression, panic attacks and itching. He confessed this hopelessness to a pastor who, to his great surprise, said, 'I don't think you're hopeless enough.' Kauflin thought he was joking, but the pastor explained, 'If you were completely hopeless, you'd stop trusting in what you think you can do to change the situation, and start trusting in what Jesus Christ has already done for you at the cross.' 'A light went on,' says Kauflin. For months afterwards, every time he felt anxious or hopeless, he would say to himself, 'I am a hopeless person, but Jesus Christ died for hopeless people.'[4]

Change is God's work

It's God himself who sanctifies us: 'May God himself, the God of peace,' prays Paul, 'sanctify you through and through' (1 Thessalonians 5:23). Other therapies can modify behaviour. Drugs can suppress the more extreme symptoms of some problems. But only God can bring true and lasting change. And that's because only God can change our hearts.

---

4 Bob Kauflin, 'Monday Devotions: The fear of man, hopelessness, and the gospel', *Worship Matters*, 16 October 2006, available at: https://worshipmatters.com/2006/10/16/monday-devotion-2.

John the Baptist said, 'I baptise you with water, but he will baptise you with the Holy Spirit' (Mark 1:8). He was talking about Jesus. John knew that he could only make people clean outwardly. But Jesus changes us on the *inside* through the Holy Spirit. He cleanses and transforms hearts. John was proclaiming the fulfilment of an Old Testament promise:

> I will sprinkle clean water on you, and you will be clean; I will cleanse you from all your impurities and from all your idols. I will give you a new heart and put a new spirit in you; I will remove from you your heart of stone and give you a heart of flesh. And I will put my Spirit in you and move you to follow my decrees and be careful to keep my laws.
> (Ezekiel 36:25–27)

Jesus does what legalism can never do: he gives us a new heart and a new spirit. Without this inner transformation, we can never please God (Romans 8:8). John Clark and Marcus Peter Johnson write:

> Loosed from the self-giving of Jesus Christ, the beauty and mystery of sanctification all too easily degenerates into technique and methodology – 'seven steps to spiritual growth' and the like – that are often little more than self-help programs designed to motivate the human spirit. On the contrary, the *Spirit*ual life of the Christian is none other than a baptism by the Spirit into Jesus Christ.[5]

People aren't changed by therapy or analysis – nor even by biblical analysis. They're changed by God, and God is in the business of change, which is achieved in three main ways.

---

5 John C. Clark and Marcus Peter Johnson, *The Incarnation of God: The mystery of the gospel as the foundation of Evangelical theology* (Wheaton, IL: Crossway, 2015), p. 178.

1 The liberating work of the Father

[Our human parents] disciplined us for a little while as they thought best; but God disciplines us for our good, in order that we may share in his holiness. No discipline seems pleasant at the time, but painful. Later on, however, it produces a harvest of righteousness and peace for those who have been trained by it.
(Hebrews 12:10–11)

God the Father is intimately involved in our lives and the purpose of that involvement is so we might 'share in his holiness'.[6] Human parents do their best to instil in their children good values and behaviour. The divine Father is engaged in the same process, but his discipline is perfect. He always 'disciplines us for our good' (v. 10). The Father is using all the circumstances of our lives to make us holy. His work in our lives, ultimately, will produce 'a harvest of righteousness and peace' (v. 11).

This doesn't mean that bad things in our lives are direct retribution for some specific misconduct. God never punishes us as Christ has already paid the price of our sin in full. God always and only disciplines to strengthen our relationship with him. It's always an act of love. It's a sign that we're truly God's children (Hebrews 12:8). God uses hardship to weaken our allegiance to this world and set our hope on the world to come; to weaken our dependence on worldly things and strengthen our faith in him (Romans 5:1–5; James 1:2–4; 1 Peter 1:6–9).

I was pruning the apple tree in my garden. Apple tree branches send shoots out in every direction. This means that shoots crisscross, getting in each other's way and making the tree less fruitful. For two hours I clambered about in the tree, creating a big pile of branches that will end up on the fire. As I was working, I couldn't help thinking of Jesus' words: 'I am the true vine, and my Father

---

6 For more on this theme, see Tim Chester, *God's Discipline: A word of encouragement in the midst of hardship* (Fearn, Ross-shire: Christian Focus, 2018).

is the gardener. He cuts off every branch in me that bears no fruit, while every branch that does bear fruit he prunes so that it will be even more fruitful' (John 15:1-2). Just as I was cutting off every shoot heading off in the wrong direction, so God cuts out every desire that does not bear good fruit. I'm hoping that the result of my pruning will be a big crop of apples. God's pruning always makes us more fruitful.

A trainee in a new workplace may be given a range of tasks and experiences to equip them with the skills they need to fulfil their role. They learn partly through being taught, partly on the job. They're exposed to difficult circumstances so that they gain experience and their confidence improves. God the Father has also designed complex and full training for each believer. Every circumstance of our life is part of this lifelong development programme. He uses 'all things' for our good, which is that we become like his Son (Romans 8:28-29). Day by day, he is working out his plan until the day we 'share in his holiness'.

2 The liberating work of the Son

What shall we say, then? Shall we go on sinning, so that grace may increase? By no means! We are those who have died to sin; how can we live in it any longer? Or don't you know that all of us who were baptised into Christ Jesus were baptised into his death? We were therefore buried with him through baptism into death in order that, just as Christ was raised from the dead through the glory of the Father, we too may live a new life.

For if we have been united with him in a death like his, we will certainly also be united with him in a resurrection like his. For we know that our old self was crucified with him so that the body ruled by sin might be done away with, that we should no longer be slaves to sin - because anyone who has died has been set free from sin.

(Romans 6:1-7)

A death and resurrection has taken place in us. Our old sin-orientated self has died. In its place we've been given a new life with new desires. The 'old self' is the person we used to be, the person we were in Adam (Romans 5:12–21). This old self was under the power of sin. We were slaves to sin. But now we've been united to Christ – a reality symbolised by baptism. We've been united with Christ in his death, his death becoming the death of our old self. And we've been united with Christ in his resurrection, which means that we've been given a new life. So Jesus not only sets us free from the *penalty* of sin = death; he also sets us free from the *reign* of sin = slavery. We're free to live for God. Telling a slave to be free is adding insult to injury, but telling a *liberated* slave to be free is an *invitation* to enjoy their new freedom and privileges.

We continue to struggle with sin. We still feel its influence. We're like a freed slave who still jumps at his old master's voice. We're like someone whose leg has healed but who still limps out of habit. We're like a former prisoner who still wakes at prison hours. That's why Paul needs to urge us, 'do not let sin reign in your mortal body so that you obey its evil desires' (Romans 6:12). Nevertheless, something decisive has happened. It's no longer inevitable that we'll sin when we face temptation. We have the power to say 'No' to temptation.

We also have a new motivation to battle with sin. We're no longer under law, we're under grace. This is counter-intuitive. People think that law and legalism are the best motives, they will get us striving for holiness. But it's grace that enables us to live for God: 'For sin shall not be your master, because you are not under the law, but under grace' (6:14). Grace wins our hearts. Sinclair Ferguson says:

> Only when we turn away from looking at our sin to look at the face of God, to find his pardoning grace, do we begin to repent. Only by seeing that there is grace and forgiveness with him would we ever dare to repent and thus return to the fellowship and presence of the Father . . . Only when grace appears on the horizon offering forgiveness will the

sunshine of the love of God melt our hearts and draw us back to him.[7]

William Romaine, one of the leaders of the Great Awakening, says,

> No sin can be crucified either in heart or life unless it first be pardoned in conscience, because there will be want of faith to receive the strength of Jesus, by whom alone it can be crucified. If it be not mortified in its guilt, it cannot be subdued in its power.[8]

We're changed when we look at Jesus, delight in Jesus, commune with Jesus. But no one will embrace Jesus if they're guilty of sin. If you're feeling guilty, then naturally you'll keep your distance from a holy God. So change only begins when we come 'under grace', with its message of divine pardon and welcome. Only then will we 'approach God's throne of grace with confidence, so that we may receive mercy and find grace to help us in our time of need' (Hebrews 4:16).

This is how my friend Matt describes his experiences at a Christian school:

> All teenagers hate rules, but this school had the most ridiculous rules. Boys had to part their hair from right to left because parting it from left to right was rebellious! They even had pictures in the school handbook with 'Christian boy' and 'rebellious boy' written under the specified hairstyles. Part your hair wrong and you got detention. And detention involved copying out entire chapters of the Bible. Trousers could not have outside seams or patch pockets. Wear the wrong trousers and you had an hour copying Psalm 119. It gets worse. In class, you weren't allowed to

---

7 Sinclair B. Ferguson, *The Christian Life: A doctrinal introduction* (Edinburgh: Banner of Truth, 1989), p. 75.

8 William Romaine, *The Life, Walk and Triumph of Faith* (Cambridge: James Clarke, 1970), p. 280.

make eye contact with other students because that was considered communication and, yep, you got Psalm 119 in detention. No chewing gum, no eating candy, no sitting with girls. Boys and girls had separate stairways and walkways. Break any of these and the psalmist would be waiting for you. These rules drove me mad. I tried to break as many as I could. In the eight months I was there, I had thirty-two detentions. They were supposed to mould my character and they did that all right: into the most rebellious kid possible! They made me angry, bitter, rebellious and rude – though I did know the psalms well!

Matt is a bouncer and he looks like one. He is big, broad, shaven-headed and doesn't have a neck. Rule on rule didn't change him. Instead, they sent him further off the rails. But you'd never guess that now. The children sit on his lap in church and he exudes a passion to tell others about Jesus. What turned his life round was the grace of Christ. What a set of rules could never do, grace did.

When Jesus talks about the Father as a gardener in John 15, he talks about himself as the vine. What gives life to branches is their connection to the vine. That connection makes them fruitful. What makes us fruitful is our connection to Jesus: 'Remain in me,' Jesus says, 'as I also remain in you. No branch can bear fruit by itself; it must remain in the vine. Neither can you bear fruit unless you remain in me' (John 15:4). If you saw a branch without grapes, you would conclude that it was dead. If you saw someone who didn't bear the fruit of holiness, then you would have good reason to suppose they weren't a true Christian. But it's not bearing fruit that makes us a Christian, any more than grapes make a vine alive. It's the other way round. The vine gives life to a branch and grapes are a sign that the branch has life from the vine. In the same way, Christ produces good works in us and our good works are a sign that we have life in him.

3 The liberating work of the Spirit

Transformation is the special work of the Holy Spirit. God chose us 'to be saved through the sanctifying work of the Spirit and through belief in the truth' (2 Thessalonians 2:13). We 'have been chosen according to the foreknowledge of God the Father, through the sanctifying work of the Spirit, to be obedient to Jesus Christ and sprinkled with his blood' (1 Peter 1:2).

There was a time when the packaging for electronic toys often had the phrase 'batteries not included' on it. As a child, you would open your long-awaited Christmas present, only to find that you couldn't make it work. The gospel is a gift that comes with 'batteries included'. God gives us power through the Holy Spirit to make our new life work. John Berridge put it like this:

> Run, John, and work, the law commands,
> Yet finds me neither feet nor hands;
> But sweeter news the gospel brings,
> It bids me fly and lends me wings.[9]

Our sanctification begins with the Spirit's work of regeneration or rebirth (John 3:3–8). The Spirit gives us new life. It's the Spirit's life in us that enables us to trust in Jesus as our Saviour (faith) and submit to Jesus as our Lord (repentance). And it's the Spirit's life in us that enables us to grow in our faith and obedience. Great Puritan John Owen puts it like this:

> Regeneration is the putting into the soul of a new, real spiritual law of life, light, holiness and righteousness, which leads to the destruction of all that hates God . . . Regeneration produces an inward miraculous change of heart . . . Our minds now have a new, saving supernatural light to enable them to think and act spiritually.[10]

Paul writes:

---

9 This verse is often attributed to John Bunyan, but is ascribed to John Berridge, a preacher during the Great Awakening, in Charles H. Spurgeon, *The Salt-cellars: Being a collection of proverbs together with homely notes thereon* (London: Passmore and Alabaster, 1889), p. 200.

10 John Owen, *The Holy Spirit*, abridged and simplified by R. J. K. Law (Edinburgh: Banner of Truth, 1998), p. 48.

> I say, live by the Spirit, and you will not gratify the desires of the flesh. For the flesh desires what is contrary to the Spirit, and the Spirit what is contrary to the flesh. They are in conflict with each other, so that you are not to do whatever you want. (Galatians 5:16–17)

The Spirit gives us the desire to do what is right and the Spirit opposes the remnants of our old self ('the flesh') when it wants to do what is wrong. Our job is to follow the Spirit. Imagine a child being taught to paint by their parent.[11] They wrap their hand round the child's, guiding each stroke of the brush. The Spirit is God's guiding hand in our lives. Whenever we want to do the wrong thing or react in the wrong way, the Spirit opposes those wrong desires. And we should be led by the Spirit. Whenever we want to do the right thing, that is the Spirit at work. And we should be led by the Spirit, even though the flesh doesn't like it. When you feel this conflict, go with the Spirit. Walk in step with the Spirit. Follow those Spirit-prompted desires.

It's as simple as that. Often I get nervous entrusting young Christians to the leading of the Spirit. I'm not sure it's good enough. I want to give them some rules as a wall round them. But that's legalism. That's why Paul reminds us, 'if you are led by the Spirit, you are not under the law' (Galatians 5:18).

Some ethical issues are complicated but, most of the time, what's wrong ('sexual immorality, impurity' and so on) and what's right ('love, joy, peace, forbearance, kindness, goodness, faithfulness, gentleness and self-control') are clear (Galatians 5:19–23). Love is the summary (Galatians 5:14). The Christian life is not as complicated as we sometimes make it. Only two commands matter: to love God and to love others (Mark 12:28–31; Romans 13:8–10). Everything else is there simply to flesh out what this love involves. The Spirit gives us a desire to love and opposes our selfish desires.

Pleasing God was supposed to be embedded in the human heart (Deuteronomy 6:6) but, in reality, it's sin that's engraved on it

---

11 J. I. Packer, *A Passion for Holiness* (Wheaton, IL: Crossway, 1992), p. 173.

(Jeremiah 17:1). So God promised to rewrite his law on our hearts through the Spirit (Jeremiah 31:31–34; Romans 7:6). The Spirit is our 'ruler'. We are like a bride who cooks lovely meals not because she is bound by some rulebook, but because of the love she has for her husband.[12] It's the Spirit who gives us this new desire for Christ and who guides us towards what pleases him through God's word: 'For God is working in you, giving you the desire and the power to do what pleases him' (Philippians 2:13, NLT).

- The Father is intimately involved in our lives so that our circumstances train us in godliness.
- The Son has set us free from both the penalty and power of sin, so that we now live under the reign of grace.
- The Spirit gives us a new attitude to sin and a new power to change.

The combined forces of the Trinity are at work in our lives to set us free and make us holy.

'Do not let your hearts be troubled.' That's what Jesus says to his disciples just after he's told them he's about to leave them as he goes to the cross (John 13:31 – 14:1). Here's a counselling session for troubled hearts. The disciples are about to face loss and fear. Their dreams are about to be nailed to a cross. So what does Jesus say in this counselling session?

He tells them that they have the Father who will love them as he has loved the Son (John 14:2–14) and the Spirit, who will accompany them as he has accompanied the Son (John 14:15–26). Jesus has more to say, but he rounds off these twin truths for troubled hearts by repeating his invitation: 'Peace I leave with you; my peace I give you. I do not give to you as the world gives. Do not let your hearts be troubled and do not be afraid' (John 14:27). And, yes, the love of God the Father and presence of God the Spirit does not look like the peace this world offers. It is not what a secular counsellor would

---

12 Marcus Honeysett, *Finding Joy: A radical rediscovery of grace* (Nottingham: IVP, 2005), pp. 65–6.

or could say to a troubled heart. But the Father's love and the Spirit's presence do calm our troubled hearts and drive away our fear.

I used to think that sanctification was a bit like pushing a boulder up a hill. It was hard, slow work and, if you lost concentration for a moment, you might find yourself back at the bottom. But it's more like rolling a boulder *down* a hill. There's something inevitable about it because it's God's work and God always succeeds. The sad thing is that, often, I try to push the boulder back up the hill. I say, in effect, 'Don't change me yet – I like doing that sin.'

Sanctified by faith

Sanctification is God's work, but we're not passive. Rather, we're active participants in the process of change. It's not that God does half the work and leaves us to do the other half. Instead, God works and we respond to his work with faith and repentance. We work hard, but then say, with Paul, 'it was not I, but the grace of God that is with me' (1 Corinthians 15:10, ESV). 'Work out your salvation with fear and trembling, for it is God who works in you to will and to act in order to fulfil his good purpose' (Philippians 2:12–13). We 'do not grow in grace by trying harder,' says Robert Kellemen, and we 'do not grow in grace by doing nothing'. Instead, we 'grow in grace by communing with God': we 'trust in the Father', 'abide in the Son' and 'yield to . . . the Spirit'.[13]

If we think the process of change is all down to us, then we're likely to slide into legalism and thence into despair. If we think it's all down to God, we'll slide into complacency and then into sin. Instead, the process of change is God's work, to which we respond. Change is a gift from God, but it's a gift that launches us into a new life of obedience. The process of change begins with God and is sustained by God. But we do not 'become passive or inactive in the face of divine grace'; we are 'energized by that grace to action.'[14]

---

13 Robert W. Kellemen, *Gospel-centered Counseling: How Christ changes lives* (Grand Rapids, MI: Zondervan, 2014), pp. 259–60.

14 John Barclay, 'By the grace of God I am what I am', in J. M. G. Barclay and Simon J. Gathercole (eds), *Divine and Human Agency in Paul and His Cultural Environment* (London: T&T Clark, 2006), p. 153.

There are important differences between justification (being right with God) and sanctification (becoming like God).[15] When someone first converts, Christ's righteousness is credited to them (Romans 4:4–8). They become, in that moment, righteous in Christ. This is what gives me confident hope regarding the day of judgement (Romans 5:1–2, 9–10), as God counts me right with him solely because of what Christ has done outside of me, without any change on my part. Sanctification, however, takes place within me. It's all about a process of gradual change. Justification is a change of my status in God's sight; sanctification is a change of my heart and character.[16] When the Bible says that we are justified by faith, it rules out any role for good works (Romans 3:27–28; 4:5). We're justified by faith *alone*. There's no room for my involvement because my justification is done and dusted at my conversion. We're also sanctified by faith, but sanctifying faith *enables* good works. Faith becomes active, 'expressing itself through love' (Galatians 5:6). So I am involved in my sanctification, as God acts in my life and I respond.

But we shouldn't separate justification and sanctification. They're joined together so that sanctification follows where justification leads. Underlying both is our union with Christ by faith. We're justified because we're united to Christ, the Righteous One. But union with Christ brings with it a change of life. Reformer John Calvin writes:

> By faith we grasp Christ's righteousness, by which alone we are reconciled to God. Yet you could not grasp this without at the same time grasping sanctification also . . . Therefore Christ justifies no one whom he does not at the same time sanctify.

---

15 For a summary of the differences between justification and sanctification, see Joel R. Beeke and Michael P. V. Barrett, *A Radical, Comprehensive Call to Holiness* (Fearn, Ross-shire: Mentor, 2021), pp. 26–7.

16 On the relationship between justification and sanctification, see J. C. Ryle, *Holiness: Its nature, hindrances, difficulties and roots* (Cambridge: James Clarke, 1956), pp. 30–1 and C. J. Mahaney, *Living the Cross Centered Life: Keeping the gospel the main thing* (Colorado Springs, CO: Multnomah, 2002), pp. 32–3.

These benefits are joined together by an everlasting and indissoluble bond.[17]

What both justification and sanctification have in common is that they take place through faith in Christ: 'The Bible teaches that we are sanctified *by faith*'.[18] By faith we find God more desirable than anything sin offers. By faith we remain in Christ, the source of our new life. By faith we embrace the new identity that is ours by grace. By faith we follow the new desires of the Spirit.

Sometimes the Reformed and Evangelical traditions treat sanctification as a human achievement, made in response to the divine act of justification. We're justified by faith in Christ's work but, it's supposed, we're sanctified by our own effort or even by law-keeping. But an emphasis on sanctification by faith, I believe, is more faithful both to the Reformed tradition and the Bible.[19] We begin the Christian life by practising faith and repentance, and we continue the Christian life by practising faith and repentance. John Owen says, 'Holiness is nothing but the implanting, writing and realising of the gospel in our souls.'[20] When the people in the crowd ask Jesus what God expects of them, he replies, 'This is the only work God wants from you: Believe in the one he has sent' (John 6:28–29, NLT).

This means that we need a kind of reconversion each day. The first of Martin Luther's famous ninety-five theses is this: 'When our Lord and Master Jesus Christ said, "Repent" (Mt 4:7), he willed the entire life of believers to be one of repentance.'[21] Each day we turn

---

17 John Calvin, *Institutes of the Christian Religion*, ed. John T. McNeill, trans. Ford Lewis Battles (Philadelphia, PA/London: Westminster/SCM Press, 1961), 3.16.1.

18 Anthony A. Hoekema, 'The Reformed perspective', *Five Views on Sanctification* (Grand Rapids, MI: Zondervan, 1987), p. 65.

19 See Henri Blocher, 'Sanctification by faith?', in Kelly M. Kapic (ed.), *Sanctification: Explorations in theology and practice* (Downers Grove, IL: IVP Academic, 2014), pp. 57–78; G. C. Berkouwer, *Faith and Sanctification* (Grand Rapids, MI: Eerdmans, 1954), pp. 32, 78, 93; and Walter Marshall, *The Gospel Mystery of Sanctification* (Grand Rapids, MI: Reformation Heritage Books, 1999), p. 28.

20 John Owen, *The Works of John Owen*, ed. William H. Goold (Edinburgh: Banner of Truth, 1965), Vol. 3, p. 370.

21 Cited in J. I. Packer, *A Passion for Holiness* (Wheaton, IL: Crossway, 1992), p. 121.

afresh in faith and repentance towards God. We rediscover our first love all over again, so that we're not tempted into spiritual adultery. The route to spiritual renewal is continually to discover and rediscover the gospel.

In Greek mythology, the Sirens would sing enchanting songs, drawing sailors irresistibly towards the rocks and certain shipwreck. Odysseus filled his crew's ears with wax and had them tie him to the mast. This is like the approach of legalism. We bind ourselves up with laws and disciplines in a vain attempt not to hear, to resist temptation. Orpheus, used a different method, playing such beautiful music on his harp that his sailors ignored the seductiveness of the Sirens' song. This is the way of faith. The grace of the gospel sings a far more glorious song than the enticements of sin, if only we have the faith to hear and listen to its music instead.

Reflection #1

Think of all the things you bring to your relationship with Christ. Create a table (see Table 1) and enter the things in either the profit column (valuable contributions to the relationship) or the loss column (worthless contributions to the relationship).

Read Philippians 3:4–9 and review what should be in the profit and loss columns. The only thing in the profit account is 'the righteousness that comes from God on the basis of faith' (v. 9).

Table 1 Valuable and worthless contributions to your relationship with Christ

Profit	Loss

Reflection #2

'God made him who had no sin to be sin for us, so that in him we might become the righteousness of God' (2 Corinthians 5:21). This verse speaks of our new status before God (justification). That status is the basis for change in our lives (sanctification). Personalise this by adding a sin with which you struggle. For example, 'God made Christ who had no *lust* to be *a porn addict* for me, so that in Christ I might become *sexually pure* before God.'

God made Christ who had no *[your sin]* to be *[what your sin makes you]* for me, so that in Christ I might become *[the opposite of your sin]* before God.

Change project

Question 3: How are you going to change?

How have you tried to change in the past?
- What actions have you taken?
- What has worked?
- What hasn't worked?

Are you trying to change yourself?
- Have you ever made vows or created lists to help you to change?
- Do you ever compare yourself to other people?
- Do you need to repent your own efforts to change?

How is God at work in your life?
- How have you changed in the past two years?
- How did that change come about?
- How can you see God at work in your life? Can you see signs of the liberating work of the Father, Son and Spirit?

How are you responding to God's work of change?

- Can you think of any ways in which you are *resisting* God's work of change in your life?
- Do you feel like you have reached a plateau in your Christian life – as though your Christian growth has levelled off? Why do you think that is?
- Are there sins with which you've struggled for many years? Do you believe you can change?

Write a summary of how you are going to change. Write down the aspect of God's work of change that especially gives you confidence that you *can* change.

4

When do you struggle?

When do you sin? In what kinds of situations do you act the wrong way or have negative feelings? What makes you depressed, angry, bitter, irritated or frustrated? When are you prone to temptation? Think about what you would like to change in your change project. Think of the last time you remember doing or feeling it. What was going on? What set you off? What wound you up? What made you depressed, angry or frustrated? Is there a pattern?

Life is tough. All of us face challenging situations. It may be a difficult family situation, sickness or financial worries. You may get wound up by your dead-end job or one of your colleagues. It may be singleness or a loveless marriage. Peer pressure may push you towards sin or the stress of having too much to do. We are messed-up people living in a messed-up world.

God cares about our struggles

'I have . . . seen . . . I have heard . . . I am concerned . . . So I have come down . . . ' That's God's message to his suffering people in Egypt (Exodus 3:7–8). Our heavenly Father sees our struggles. He hears our cries for help. He's concerned about what we're going through. We often think that no one knows or no one cares, but God knows and God cares. We're allowed to struggle. It's legitimate to feel pain, disappointment and heartache. Many of the psalms talk about struggle and, by talking about it, they give it a home in God's word. God the Father sees our struggles.

But God doesn't just look on our struggles from a distance. He has rolled up his sleeves, come down, got stuck in, experienced our struggles at first hand. God entered our world when the Son of God became human. Jesus knows what it is to be hungry, assaulted, rejected, tired, lonely, tempted, needy, opposed, busy. He faced poverty, injustice, temptation and betrayal. More than all that, on the cross he felt forsaken by his father (Mark 15:34). Jesus has shared our struggles. Jesus wasn't a special being floating above all the mess. We mustn't have a Sunday school picture of Jesus dressed in a sparkling white robe, surrounded by happy children. He was a real person, living in a world of dirt, pain and frustration.

'I'm not talking to them about it – they won't understand,' we sometimes say. 'Nobody knows what it's like to be me.' But God does know what it's like. Jesus fully shared our humanity and, 'Because he himself suffered when he was tempted, he is able to help those who are being tempted' (Hebrews 2.18)). He is able to 'feel sympathy for our weaknesses' and so we can 'approach God's throne of grace with confidence, so that we receive mercy and find grace to help us in our time of need' (4:14–16).

Not only has God experienced our struggles but he is also with us through the Spirit here and now. God says,

> Do not fear, for I have redeemed you; I have summoned you by name; you are mine. When you pass through the waters, I will be with you; and when you pass through the rivers, they will not sweep over you. When you walk through the fire, you will not be burned; the flames will not set you ablaze.
> (Isaiah 43:1–2)

On the night before he died, Jesus said to his disciples, 'I will ask the Father, and he will give you another Counsellor to be with you for ever – the Spirit of Truth' (John 14:16–17, NIV 1984). People sometimes tell me that they need a counsellor and ask if I have any recommendations. Often another Christian can help us to understand what's going on in our hearts, but we have the great Counsellor already, we have the Spirit of Truth. And Jesus says that he is with us for ever. The word Jesus uses to describe the Spirit has the ideas of counsellor and comforter all rolled up into one. Jesus goes on to say:

the Advocate, the Holy Spirit, whom the Father will send in my name, will teach you all things and will remind you of everything I have said to you. Peace I leave with you; my peace I give you. I do not give to you as the world gives. Do not let your hearts be troubled and do not be afraid.
(John 14:26–27)

Jesus gives us peace by giving us the Holy Spirit as our Counsellor, to point us towards God's gracious promises. Jesus isn't being naive, nor is he promising an easy ride. Later he says, 'In this world you will have trouble' (16:33). We will have *troubled circumstances*, but we don't need to have *troubled hearts*. Why not? Because we have a Divine Comforter who reminds us of the truth.

God does something about our struggles

I sat opposite her. Her face was puffy and red after many hours crying. The man she had hoped to marry had just died in an accident. There was faith, but also questions and a lot of grief.

I count it a great privilege to be with people at times of crisis in their lives. We go many layers beyond superficial to the deep things of the heart. But being with her was pretty much all I could offer. I couldn't bring him back, nor heal the wound in her heart.

Having someone with us is a great comfort in the valley of the shadow of death. But God does so much more than just put an arm round our shoulders.

First, God uses our struggles. 'We know that in all things God works for the good of those who love him . . . to be conformed to the likeness of his Son' (Romans 8:28–29). It's easy to believe that when good things happen to us. It's not so easy to believe when the bad things come our way. But the Bible is clear that God uses suffering to make us like Jesus. Evil is evil. It's painful, confusing and real. Behind it is the malevolent mind of Satan. But God uses it for his bigger purposes (Genesis 50:20; Acts 4:27–28). For all eternity, your past experience of evil will enhance your eternal experience of glory (2 Corinthians 4:17). You'll be shaped by it in beautiful ways:

> we also rejoice in our sufferings, because we know that suffering produces perseverance; perseverance, character; and character, hope. And hope does not disappoint us.
> (Romans 5:3b–5, NIV 1984)

> Consider it pure joy, my brothers and sisters, whenever you face trials of many kinds, because you know that the testing of your faith produces perseverance. Let perseverance finish its work so that you may be mature and complete, not lacking anything.
> (James 1:2–4)

> In all this [hope] you greatly rejoice, though now for a little while you may have had to suffer grief in all kinds of trials. These have come so that the proven genuineness of your faith – of greater worth than gold, which perishes even though refined by fire – may result in praise, glory and honour when Jesus Christ is revealed.
> (1 Peter 1:6–7)

What's striking about these passages is the way that they all begin with a call to rejoice. We can rejoice in suffering when we make the connection between suffering and growth. Sometimes we see it in our lives; sometimes we can hold on to this truth only by faith. But we rejoice because we trust that God is using all things for our good – the good of becoming like Jesus.

Second, God not only uses our struggles but he also promises to bring them to an end. He has taken our sufferings on himself to end them. On the cross, Jesus took God's wrath on himself in our place, freeing us from God's curse. He promises a new world, without sin or pain. His resurrection is the beginning of a new creation that will come to completion at the end of history – a new creation in which God himself will 'wipe every tear' and in which 'There will be no more death or mourning or crying or pain' (Revelation 21:3–4).

You can crop a photo on your phone. You simply click the 'edit' option in your app and select 'crop'. The picture is surrounded by lines that you can drag inwards to remove any unwanted areas around the edge of the photo. But you can't crop *outwards*. You can't drag those lines out to include content that wasn't in the original photo.

But it's different with the gospel. The gospel enables us to crop outwards. When we think about our struggles, we often paint a picture in which they are front and centre. But the gospel enables us to pull the line around this picture out to the left to reveal the cross – the great demonstration of God's love and Christ's redemption. Pull the line to the right and we see a new creation, in which everything has been made right. Pull it a bit further and we begin to see an eternity of glory that awaits those who remain true to Christ. Pull the line at the top up and we see a generous Father who cares for his people. Sometimes we can change our circumstances – get a new job, repair a broken relationship, fight our way back to health. But not always. Some things are beyond our power to change. Even then, we can always see the bigger picture of God's love and the future that he promises to his children.

Our struggles reveal our hearts

Why do we do the things we do? Why do we get angry, frustrated, irritable or depressed – or, for that matter, happy, excited or content? Why do we lie, steal, fight and gossip? Why do we dream, fantasise, envy and plot? Why do we overwork or overeat? Why do children misbehave? Why do adults have sex outside marriage? Why do we worry about what people think? Why do we fail to be the parent, spouse or employee we should be? Why do we speak when we shouldn't and keep quiet when we should speak up? Where do evil thoughts, sexual immorality, theft, murder, adultery, greed, malice all come from? Jesus gives us the answer: 'it is from within, out of a person's heart, that evil thoughts come – sexual immorality, theft, murder, adultery, greed, malice, deceit, lewdness, envy, slander, arrogance and folly. All these evils come from inside and defile a person' (Mark 7:21–23).

My behaviour comes from my heart

From within. Out of a person's heart. From inside. According to the Bible, *the source of all human behaviour and emotions is the heart.* The 'heart' in the Bible means more than the organ that pumps blood round the body. It refers to the inner person or your essential self. It's shorthand for our thinking and desires. The heart 'includes everything that we ascribe to the head and brains – power of perception, reason, understanding, insight, consciousness, memory, knowledge, judgment, sense of direction, discernment.'[1]

The root cause of my behaviour is always, always my heart. 'As water reflects the face,' says Proverbs 27:19, 'so one's life reflects the heart.' Gary Millar describes the heart as the 'hidden control centre of the whole human being'.[2] People like to think that they are in control of their behaviour, as though their will is at the helm of their lives. Or they think of themselves as rational people, as though the mind is at the helm. But the Bible says that we're driven by what we love or desire. I love what historian Ashley Null says about Thomas Cranmer, the great reforming Archbishop of Canterbury. Null says, 'For Cranmer, love lies at the root of everything. *What the heart loves, the will chooses and the mind justifies.*'[3] In other words, we do what we want to do, then we come up with reasons to justify our behaviour.

What we see is behaviour and emotions, so it's easy to focus our energies on trying to change them. But lasting change is only achieved by tackling their source – the heart. Jesus says:

No good tree bears bad fruit, nor does a bad tree bear good fruit. Each tree is recognised by its own fruit. People do not pick figs from thorn-bushes, or grapes from briers. A good man brings good things out of the good stored up in his heart,

---

1 H.-W. Wolff, *Anthropology of the Old Testament* (London: SCM Press, 1974), p. 51.

2 J. Gary Millar, *Changed into His Likeness: A biblical theology of personal transformation* (London: IVP, 2021), p. 44.

3 Ashley Null, Foreword to Winfield Bevins, *Our Common Prayer: A field guide to the Book of Common Prayer* (Simeon Press, 2013), pp. 13–14.

and an evil man brings evil things out of the evil stored up in his heart. For the mouth speaks what the heart is full of. (Luke 6:43–45)

If you see a bush with thorns, you know that it's not a fig tree. It has the DNA of a thorn bush and it's this DNA that causes it to grow thorns rather than figs. It's the same with people. Our sinful behaviour reflects the sin in our hearts. Every sinful action and negative emotion reveals a problem in our hearts.

When I left home aged nineteen, my father gave me a verse: 'Above all else, guard your heart, for everything you do flows from it' (Proverbs 4:23). Sadly, it took me twenty years to realise what an important verse that is. All our actions flow from the heart.

Our circumstances trigger our hearts

Only when we understand the role of our hearts can we truly understand the role of our circumstances in sin. Our struggles and temptations often trigger sin, but they never cause it. The root cause is always our heart and its sinful desires. We choose how we respond to circumstances and what determines those choices are the thinking and desires of our hearts.

People don't see it like this. Think of the last time you were angry. Not all anger is bad. God himself is angry about sin. 'Good anger' is an emotional response to the right things (sin and injustice) in the right way (a controlled response that pursues good). But think about the last time you were angry in a destructive way. What made you angry? We normally point to external factors: 'They didn't treat me with respect.' 'Someone smashed my car.' 'They never see it my way.' But James says that what causes fights and quarrels are 'your desires that battle within you' (James 4:1–2). Anger arises because my desires are thwarted or threatened. External pressures always have an impact on our behaviour *via our hearts*. We can't blame our circumstances.

When tempted, no one should say, 'God is tempting me.' For God cannot be tempted by evil, nor does he tempt anyone; but

each person is tempted when they are dragged away by their own evil desire and enticed. Then, after desire has conceived, it gives birth to sin; and sin, when it is full-grown, gives birth to death.
(James 1:13–15)

James is talking to Christians facing 'trials of many kinds' (1:2b). If we persevere under trial, God will reward us with 'the crown of life' (v. 12b). What we *can't* do is blame God for our being in this situation. It's not God's fault if I fail to persevere. I can't say, 'It was my upbringing, my biology, my personal history or my circumstances.' No, James tells us that what causes a person to be enticed by temptation is 'their own evil desire' (v. 14b). Desires lead to sin, says James, and sin leads to death. The deadly effects of sin on our lives, emotions and relationships stem from the evil desires of our hearts. Jerry Bridges warns against using the language of 'defeat' to describe sin. It suggests being overwhelmed by external factors and can therefore suggest that we ourselves are not to blame. The language of 'disobedience' more accurately describes what's happening.[4]

Our background can *shape* our sinful response. Some people express anger through foot-stamping and shouting; others opt for silence and withdrawal. Whether you fly into a rage or withdraw may depend on your upbringing, on what you've 'learned' from people around you. But both rage and silence are anger, and the root cause of that anger lies in our hearts.

If you saw me in my study at 7:30 in the morning, reading my Bible or praying, you might think me a godly man. There I am: calm, peaceful, trusting. But observe me half an hour later as I attempt to marshal my daughters out the door for school and you'd see a man who's far from godly. I used to think of myself as that calm, gentle person – the 7:30 me – and concluded I was pretty godly too! If I'm provoked to sin, then the problem must be whatever provoked me (in this case, my recalcitrant daughters). But I've

---

4 Jerry Bridges, *The Pursuit of Holiness* (Colorado Springs. CO: NavPress, 1978), pp. 84–5.

had to face the fact that the real me is the 8:00 me – the person revealed when the sinful desires of my heart are exposed by trying circumstances and annoying people. It's the real me who is revealed when I'm too tired to keep up the pretence.

There's an important clarification to add at this stage. The fact that suffering often reveals the idols of your heart does *not* necessarily mean your suffering is your fault. Suffering may *expose* sinful desires, but that doesn't mean those sinful desires *caused* your suffering. Of course it's possible – our selfishness and pride can wreak all sorts of havoc in our lives and relationships. But there's not an *inevitable* link between your suffering and some sin in your life. That's the point Jesus makes in John 9, when he meets a man blind from birth. The disciples can't work out whether the man's blindness is due to his sin or his parents' sin. But Jesus rejects their underlying assumption that his blindness must be the result of some specific sin. "'Neither this man nor his parents sinned,'" said Jesus, "but this happened so that the works of God might be displayed in him'" (John 9:1–3).

There are two contrasting dangers for us as we respond to suffering, especially when it involves some form of conflict. You may need someone outside the situation to help you to navigate between these two dangers.

1 **Putting our guilt on to other people** We can adopt a victim mentality in which we blame other people for our problems, but if we avoid taking responsibility in this way, then we'll not repent. If we don't repent, then we'll not move on towards freedom and change.
2 **Taking other people's guilt on to ourselves** It's all too possible that we will be made to feel like we're to blame when, in fact, the fault lies wholly or primarily with others. People may tell us that we're the problem to avoid attention falling on their own actions. While we're to humble ourselves before God, we're not to let other people be our judge or live under their verdict against us.

We sin because we do not trust God and do not worship God

Whether we share most, some or none of the blame for our suffering, our *response* to it often *reveals* our heart. That means our struggles are a great opportunity to purify our hearts.

So what is it that's going on within us? The Bible says that two things are always happening in our hearts. Hebrews 4:12 speaks of 'the thoughts and attitudes of the heart':

- we think, interpret, believe, trust
- we desire, worship, want, treasure.

Human beings are always interpreters and always worshippers. We're interpreters who form explanations for what's happening to us. And we were made by God to worship him, so worship is hard-wired into our being.

So there is a twofold problem in our heart:

1 what we think or trust
2 what we desire or worship.

All our actions – the good, the bad and the ugly – are the result of the way our thoughts and desires shape our will or behaviour. And those actions turn bad when our thoughts and desires go wrong. We sin when we don't *trust* God above everything (when we think in the wrong way) and when we don't *desire* God above everything (when we worship the wrong thing). Sin happens when we believe lies about God instead of trusting God's word and when we worship idols instead of worshipping God. Listen to Ed Welch:

> Any violation of God's law is an expression of the heart, as is faith and obedience. Our emotions are also, more often than not, animated by the orientation of our hearts. When our worship is true, we experience joy, peace, love, and hope,

even in difficult situations. When our worship is false, and the things we desire are unattainable or impotent, we can be grieved, bitter, depressed, angry, or fearful. Our emotions usually *mean* something, and it is wise to ask, 'What are my emotions saying?' 'What are they pointing to?'[5]

Destructive or sinful behaviours (lying, manipulation, violence, theft, adultery, addictions and eating disorders) and negative or sinful emotions (worry, envy, guilt, bitterness and pride) all arise when our hearts don't trust God as we should and we don't worship God as we should. So the answer is faith and repentance. We need to:

- trust God instead of believing lies = faith
- worship God instead of worshipping idols = repentance.

The key is to make the link between our specific sins and the lies and idols in our hearts. Doing so enables us to turn from those lies in faith and to turn from our idols in repentance. This is what we'll explore in the following chapters.

Reflection #1

The heart is the home of our principles and the foundation of our actions . . . The greatest difficulty in conversion is to win the heart to God; and the greatest difficulty after conversion is to keep the heart with God . . . The heart is the source of all vital operations. It is the spring and origin of both good and evil just as the spring in a watch sets all the wheels in motion. The heart is the warehouse; the hand and tongue are just the shops. What is in the hand and tongue comes from the warehouse of the heart. The other parts of

---

5 Edward T. Welch, *Addictions: A banquet in the grave* (Phillipsburg, NJ: P&R Publishing, 2001), pp. 129–30.

the body only put into effect what the heart first contrives (Luke 6:45). So if our heart is not right then our actions will go wrong.[6]

Reflection #2

How would you complete the following statements:

- when I get angry, it's usually because . . .
- when I get despondent, it's usually because . . .
- when I disobey God, it's usually because . . .

Think about your answers. Do they describe what triggers your behaviour or the root cause of your behaviour? Do they describe what's going on in your heart?

Change project

Question 4: When do you struggle?

What are your struggles?
- What pressures do you face regularly?
- Who are the people you find difficult to cope with?
- What situations cause you to worry or get angry or brood or overreact or dream of revenge or justify yourself or become despondent?
- What did you think or believe in those moments?
- What did you want or worship in those moments?
- Can you see how God is using your trials?

---

6   Adapted from John Flavel, *Keeping the Heart* (Fearn, Ross-shire: Christian Heritage, 1999), pp. 7 and 10.

When do you struggle with the issue you've chosen for your change project?

- When do you often do it or feel it?
- What triggers it?
- Are there any patterns?
- What do you think or believe in those moments?
- What do you want or worship in those moments?

What's going on in your heart?

- What did you want, desire or wish for?
- What did you fear? What were you worrying about?
- What did you think you needed?
- What were your strategies and intentions designed to accomplish?
- What or whom were you trusting?
- Whom were you trying to please? Whose opinion of you counted?
- What were you loving? What were you hating?
- What would have brought you the greatest happiness, pleasure or delight? What would have brought you the greatest pain and misery?[7]

Write a summary of when you sin and what is going on in your heart.

We'll be thinking more about what's going on in our hearts in the next chapters.

---

7 From Elyse Fitzpatrick, *Idols of the Heart: Learning to long for God alone* (Phillipsburg, NJ: P&R Publishing, 2001), p. 163.

5

What truths do you need to turn to?

Lee had panic attacks. In time they became self-reinforcing: the fear of an attack would induce one. He would phone me three or four times a week. Each time I would speak the truth to him. We developed some catchphrases. 'God is greater than your thoughts.' 'Not "What if?" but "What is" and what is, is that God is in control.' The truth set him free. The truth of God's sovereignty brought peace, and with it a new realisation of the centrality of God and his glory. It wasn't instantaneous. Each day brought a fresh struggle to believe. Another of our catchphrases was, 'Yesterday was a victory, today is another battle.' But in time the panic attacks went away.

We find true freedom by embracing God's reign over our lives, and trusting his reign to be wise and good. This is the interpretation of life that brings joy and peace. In the garden of Eden, the Serpent persuaded Eve to doubt this and the goodness of God's rule. Satan offered a different world view, portraying God as a tyrant whose rule should be rejected. Eve took the fruit because she believed this lie about God. Sin began with humanity disbelieving God's word.

Behind every sin is a lie

Sinful acts always have their origin in some form of unbelief. Behind every sin is a lie. As we've seen, the root of all our behaviour and emotions is the heart – what it trusts and what it treasures. And people are given over to sinful desires because 'They exchanged the truth about God for a lie' (Romans 1:24–25).

66

So I tell you this, and insist on it in the Lord, that you must no longer live as the Gentiles do, in the futility of their thinking. They are darkened in their understanding and separated from the life of God because of the ignorance that is in them due to the hardening of their hearts. Having lost all sensitivity, they have given themselves over to sensuality so as to indulge in every kind of impurity, and they are full of greed.
(Ephesians 4:17–19)

Humanity's problem is futile thinking, darkened understanding and ignorant hearts. This is the cause of indulgence, impurity and lust. We sin because we believe the lie that we are better off without God – that his rule is oppressive, we will be free without him and sin offers more than God. This is true of every sin.

Often, we can identify specific lies behind specific sinful acts and emotions. I may envy, steal or be anxious about money because I believe the lie that consumer goods give meaning to my life or because I believe God doesn't care for me. I may commit adultery or get depressed about my singleness because I believe the lie that intimacy with another person will give me more than God can give. Puritan pastor Richard Baxter put it well: 'The will never desires evil as evil, but as something that seems good.'[1] So, when most of us choose to sin, it's not because we think an evil life is better than a good life; it's because we mistakenly think it's this sinful course of action that will lead to a good life.

Of course, not many people think of themselves as believing lies! But every time we don't trust God's word, we're believing something else – and that something is always a lie. If I get angry when I'm stuck in traffic, it's because I don't trust God. I believe the lie that God isn't in control or that his purposes for me are not good. If I overwork, it's because I don't trust God – perhaps because I believe the lie that I need to prove or justify myself. This is a radical

---

1 Richard Baxter, *A Christian Directory* (Philadelphia, PA: Soli Deo Gloria: 1997), p. 85, modernised.

view of sin. It means some (though not all) of our negative emotions are sinful because they're symptoms of unbelief, which is the greatest sin and the root of sin. If we're depressed or bitter, it may be because we believe that God isn't being good to us or he's not in control. 'Everything that does not come from faith is sin,' says Paul in Romans 14:23b.

Not many Christians think of themselves as non-believers. After all, we may use this term to describe people who aren't Christians at all. Most of us can happily sign up to the creeds of our church. But then our problems rarely arise from disbelief in a confessional or theoretical sense, though this may sometimes be the case. More often, our problems arise from functional or practical disbelief. Our problems emerge from the gap between what we believe in theory and what we believe in practice. On Sunday morning, I sing of my belief in justification by faith (confessional faith), but on Monday morning, I still feel the need to prove myself (functional disbelief). I may believe I'll be acquitted on the day of judgement, but still want to justify myself in an argument tomorrow. I may affirm that God is sovereign (confessional faith), but still get anxious when I can't control my life (functional disbelief). Sanctification is the progressive narrowing of the gap between our confessional faith and functional faith.

The truth shall set you free

Recognising that behind every sin is a lie not only gives us a radical view of sin, it also points us to the road out of sinful behaviour and emotions. That road is trust in God.

> The path of the righteous is like the morning sun,
> shining ever brighter till the full light of day.
> But the way of the wicked is like deep darkness;
> they do not know what makes them stumble.
>
> My son, pay attention to what I say;
> turn your ear to my words.
> Do not let them out of your sight,

keep them within your heart;
for they are life to those who find them
    and health to one's whole body.
Above all else, guard your heart,
    for everything you do flows from it.
(Proverbs 4:18–23)

Proverbs describes the road of trust in God as being like the first gleam of dawn. Maybe you feel like you're in darkness, trapped in your behaviour, with negative emotions weighing heavily on you. Seeing them as symptoms of unbelief can be like the first ray of light in the darkness, a dawn. Hope begins with the realisation that the answer is to be found by looking to God. It's a long road that takes a lifetime to travel, but with every step, the light of God's goodness shines 'ever brighter till the full light of day' (v. 18). We follow this road by paying attention to the word of God (vv. 20–21). God's word is our road map. The gracious promises of God give true life and health (v. 22). The truth will guard our hearts and therefore our lives (v. 23).

This is what the LORD says:

'Cursed is the one who trusts in man,
    who draws strength from mere flesh
    and whose heart turns away from the LORD.
That person will be like a bush in the wastelands;
    they will not see prosperity when it comes.
They will dwell in the parched places of the desert,
    in a salt land where no one lives.

'But blessed is the one who trusts in the LORD,
    whose confidence is in him.
They will be like a tree planted by the water
    that sends out its roots by the stream.
It does not fear when heat comes;
    its leaves are always green.

It has no worries in a year of drought
   and never fails to bear fruit.'
(Jeremiah 17:5–8)

Jeremiah uses a different picture. People who trust in their own strength are like barren shrubs in a desert. Maybe that's how you feel – as though you are running on empty, thirsty for something more. Life feeling fruitless and pointless. God says that people who trust in him are like trees planted by water, never failing to bear fruit. That doesn't mean they have an easy life. They feel the scorching heat just as much as anyone else. But their roots go down deep into the refreshing waters of God's word. Faith in God sustains them and keeps them fruitful in the midst of adversity.

'Everyone who sins is a slave to sin,' says Jesus (John 8:34). People feel trapped in their negative behaviour or emotions. They feel like they can't change and, in one sense, they can't. Trying to change behaviour alone doesn't work because the lies that create the behaviour are still there. But Jesus says, 'If you hold to my teaching, you are really my disciples. Then you will know the truth, and the truth will set you free' (8:31b–32).

Just as lies about God lead to the slavery of sin, so the truth about God leads to the freedom of service (Galatians 5:1, 13). The truth that sets us free is the gospel ('If you hold to my teaching', John 8:31). Freedom is found in the truth that we were made to worship God, to serve God, to trust God. Freedom is found in acknowledging that we are responsible for the mess we've made of our lives, that our problems are rooted in our hearts, we deserve God's judgement and we desperately need God. Freedom is found in accepting that God is in control of our lives, he is gracious and he forgives those who come to him in faith. Paul says, 'For the grace of God has appeared that offers salvation to all people. It teaches us to say "No" to ungodliness and worldly passions, and to live self-controlled, upright and godly lives' (Titus 2:11–12).

Often we can be specific about the truth that will set us free from the lies enslaving us. If I'm enslaved by my worries, then freedom is found in trusting the sovereign care of my heavenly Father. If I'm enslaved by the need to prove myself, then freedom is found in trusting that I'm fully justified in God's sight through the atoning work of Christ.

Seeing, knowing, embracing, desiring

Change takes place as we see the glory of God in Jesus, as we know the truth that sets us free. But 'seeing' and 'knowing' don't capture the force of the understanding that we need. When this chapter asks what truths you need to turn to, it doesn't mean simply acquiring information or agreeing with statements. It's possible to see without seeing (Jeremiah 5:21; Ezekiel 12:2; Matthew 13:13). Nineteenth-century theologian Charles Hodge says that true knowledge of Christ 'is not the apprehension of what he is, simply by the intellect, but also . . . involves . . . the corresponding feeling of adoration, delight, desire and contentment'.[2] Seeing and knowing Christ isn't just receiving information but also recognising him as the Altogether Lovely One. It's embracing the truth about God and delighting in it.

Psalm 19:10 says that the truth of God's word is 'sweeter than honey'. However, suppose you've never tasted honey. You know it's sweet because you've heard that it is from reliable sources. But that's a very different kind of knowledge from taking a big spoonful and falling in love with its sweetness ourselves.[3] We need to 'taste and see that the LORD is good' (Psalm 34:8, ESV).

Paul prays that 'the eyes of your heart may be enlightened in order that you may know the hope to which he has called you, the riches of his glorious inheritance in his holy people' (Ephesians 1:17–18). Our prayer should be that we will not only comprehend truth with the eyes of our mind but also embrace truth with 'the eyes of [our] heart' (v. 18). This is the key to change. Puritan Walter Marshall says, 'The more good and beneficial we

---

2 Cited in John Piper, *When I Don't Desire God: How to fight for God* (Wheaton, IL: Crossway, 2004), p. 17.

3 This analogy is from a sermon by Jonathan Edwards called 'A divine and supernatural light', in *The Works of Jonathan Edwards* (London: Ball, Arnold & Co., 1840), Vol. 2, pp. 12–17.

apprehend God to us to all eternity, doubtless the more lovely God will be to us, and our affections will be the more inflamed towards him.'[4]

- Seeing God ⇨ delighting in God ⇨ desiring God ⇨ desiring God more than we desire sin.

Preaching to our hearts

We need to become preachers. We need to learn to preach to our own hearts. The psalmist says, 'Praise the LORD, my soul, and forget not all his benefits' (Psalm 103:2). But to whom is he speaking? The answer is *to himself*. Famous preacher Martyn Lloyd-Jones said, 'Have you realised that most of your unhappiness in life is due to the fact that you are listening to yourself instead of talking to yourself?'[5] We need to take every thought captive (2 Corinthians 10:3–5).

Our problem, says Sinclair Ferguson, is that 'we think with our feelings'.[6] We don't always *feel* joy in God but, by faith, we can tell ourselves that he *is* our joy. When we find ourselves tempted to sinful behaviour or when we find that our emotions are getting the better of us, we need to speak truth to our hearts. Say the truth to yourself repeatedly so that it sinks in: 'God is all I need.' Say it slowly: 'God . . . is . . . all . . . I . . . need.' Say it out loud. Say it back to him: 'You are all I need'.

It helps if you can identify the specific lies behind your sin and the corresponding truths that will set you free. But you don't have to be able to analyse your heart in detail. It's the truth of the gospel that brings change. This is how John Newton describes the liberating power of Jesus' name in his hymn:[7]

---

4   Walter Marshall, *The Gospel Mystery of Sanctification*, ed. Joel R. Beeke (Grand Rapids, MI: Reformation Heritage Books, 1999), p. 23.

5   D. Martyn Lloyd-Jones, *Spiritual Depression: Its causes and cure* (London: Pickering & Inglis, 1965), p. 20.

6   Sinclair Ferguson, cited in C. J. Mahaney, *Living the Cross Centered Life: Keeping the gospel the main thing* (Colorado Springs, CO: Multnomah, 2002), p. 48.

7   'How sweet the name of Jesus sounds', 1779.

How sweet the name of Jesus sounds
in a believer's ear!
It soothes his sorrows, heals his wounds
and drives away his fear.

It makes the wounded spirit whole
and calms the troubled breast;
'tis manna to the hungry soul
and to the weary, rest.

Dear name! the rock on which we build,
our shield and hiding place,
our never-failing treasury, filled
with boundless stores of grace.

The four Gs

I want to identify four life-changing truths about God. Psalm 62:11–12 (ESV) says, 'Once God has spoken; twice have I heard this: that power belongs to God, and that to you, O Lord, belongs steadfast love.' The key truths that God declares about himself are his *greatness* and *glory* ('that power belongs to God', v. 11) and his *goodness* and *grace* ('that to you, O Lord, belongs steadfast love', v. 12).

1 God is great – so we do not have to be in control.
2 God is glorious – so we do not have to fear others.
3 God is good – so we do not have to look elsewhere.
4 God is gracious – so we do not have to prove ourselves.

There's much more to be said about God than is covered by these four truths, but they offer a powerful diagnostic tool for addressing most of the sins and emotions with which we struggle. Over the years, they've become known as 'the four Gs'.[8]

---

8 For worked-through examples of how the four Gs apply to various areas of life, see Tim Chester, *The Busy Christian's Guide to Busyness* (Nottingham: IVP, 2006); Tim Chester and Ed Moll, *Gospel Centered Family: Becoming the parents God wants you to be* (Epsom: The Good Book Company, 2009), p. 29; Tim Chester, *Captured by a Better Vision: Living Porn-Free*

1 God is great – so we do not have to be in control

Travelling at the speed of light (186,000 miles a second), you would encircle the earth seven times in one second and go past the moon in two seconds. At this speed, it would take you 4.3 years to reach our nearest star and 100,000 years to cross our galaxy. There are thought to be at least a hundred million galaxies in the universe. It would take two million light years to reach the next closest galaxy and twenty million to reach the next cluster of galaxies. And you will still have only just begun to explore the universe.

All this was created when God simply spoke a word. In fact, Isaiah tells us that he marked off the heavens with the breadth of his hand (Isaiah 40:12). It's a spatial metaphor for God, who exists outside of space, but it gives us a sense of the scale of God: the whole universe fits in his hand. Hold your hand up: the entire universe is that big to God! Hebrews 1:3 says that Jesus sustains it all by the power of his word. He 'works out everything in conformity with the purpose of his will' (Ephesians 1:11). In a mysterious way that involves human freedom, God orders every event and determines every action. 'The king's heart is in the hand of the LORD; he directs it like a watercourse wherever he pleases' (Proverbs 21:1, NIV 1984). Even evil actions are part of his plan. The conspiracy that sent Jesus to the cross was the result of evil choices by human beings. Yet 'they did what [God's] power and will had decided beforehand should happen' (Acts 4:28). From the movement of atoms to the complexities of human history, God sustains all and rules all.

I wonder if you've ever lost work on a computer because it crashed. It happened to me. I let out a loud 'Nnoooo!' as my head dropped down to my desk. To whom was I speaking? The reality is, though I might not have admitted it, that I was crying out a 'No' to God and his sovereignty. I was rejecting his sovereign rule over my life. 'No, God, you don't know best. Your rule is *not* good.'

(Nottingham: IVP, 2010); Tim Chester, *Gospel Centered Work: Becoming the worker God wants you to be* (Epsom: The Good Book Company, 2013), pp. 39–62; Tim Chester and Marcus Honeysett, *Gospel Centred Preaching: Becoming the preacher God wants you to be* (Epsom: The Good Book Company, 2014), pp. 56–8; and Tim Chester, *Mission Matters: Love says go*, Keswick Foundations Series (Nottingham: IVP, 2015), pp. 129–42.

Alan is sitting on a train. Inexplicably, it's stopped just outside the station. He's getting very angry because it looks like he'll miss his hospital appointment.

Beth's worried. Replacing their car has wiped out their savings. She's worried about whether they'll have enough money left at the end of the month. When her husband comes home with an expensive-looking bunch of flowers to cheer her up, she just bursts into tears.

Colin's feeling very frustrated. He's trying to get a new community project going, but everything seems to be going wrong. As a result, he's becoming irritable with his kids.

Dorothy's lying awake at night, thinking about her friend Eileen. Dorothy's noticed what seem to be symptoms of postnatal depression. She's looked after Eileen's baby a couple of times, but has her own responsibilities. She wishes there was more she could do for her friend.

In Mark 4:35 – 5:43, Jesus displays his control over the natural world, over the spirit world, over sickness and even over death. The stories are told to highlight Jesus' complete authority. He brings a girl back from death as easily as you or I might rouse someone from sleep (5:41). All the time, Mark presents the alternatives of fear and faith. The disciples are afraid in the storm. Among them were experienced fishermen, so this was no irrational phobia, yet Jesus rebukes them, 'Why are you so afraid? Do you still have no faith?' (4:40). The people see a formerly demon-possessed man in his right mind and fear the power that tamed him (5:15). A sick woman comes before Jesus 'trembling with fear' (v. 33), but Jesus speaks a word of peace to her (v. 34). Because of her faith, she has no need to fear God. Jesus' word to Jairus is the punchline of this section: 'Don't be afraid; just believe' (v. 36).

God is greater than all the things we fear. The stories don't teach that we'll never face sickness or death. Instead, they teach us that we needn't fear the circumstances of life because God is in control. He works to the good for us in every circumstance. He'll bring us safely home to glory. Death is not the last word: the last word is 'Talitha koum!' – 'rise up' (5:41).

What happens when you don't truly trust in God's sovereign control? You might try to take control yourself in harmful ways, through manipulation or domination. You might wear yourself out with busyness or frustration. You might make your security and wealth a bigger priority than God's kingdom. Or you might worry (Philippians 4:6–7). We become preoccupied with our bills, then money becomes our main obsession. All because we don't believe that our Father knows what we need (Luke 12:22–31). Jesus goes straight to the heart of the problem: our little faith.

> 'Who of you by worrying can add a single hour to his life? . . . you of little faith! And do not set your heart on what you will eat or drink; do not worry about it. For the pagan world runs after all such things, and your Father knows that you need them. But seek his kingdom, and these things will be given to you as well.'
> (Luke 12:25–31)

We often associate the sovereignty of God with theological debates, but for all of us it's a daily practical choice. For me, the issue is escapism. I have to choose between a fantasy world in which I'm sovereign and the real world in which God is sovereign. I have to choose between my false sovereignty and God's real sovereignty. When I feel like running away, I have to choose to find refuge in God.

2 God is glorious – so we do not have to fear others

One common reason for our sin is that we crave the approval of people or we fear their rejection. We 'need' the acceptance of others and so we're controlled by them. The Bible's term for this is the 'fear of man': 'Fear of man will prove to be a snare, but whoever trusts in the LORD is kept safe' (Proverbs 29:25). In his book *When People Are Big and God Is Small*, Ed Welch says that the 'fear of man' has many symptoms: susceptibility to peer pressure; 'needing' something from a spouse; a concern with self-esteem; being over-committed because we can't say 'No'; fear of being exposed; telling small lies to make ourselves look good; people making us jealous, angry, depressed or anxious; avoiding people; comparing ourselves to others; and fear of evangelism.[9]

Our culture tries to overcome this problem by finding ways to bolster self-esteem, but this actually compounds the problem. We become dependent on whatever or whoever will boost it. In reality, low self-esteem is thwarted pride – we don't have the status that we think we deserve. We elevate often good desires (for love, affirmation, respect) to needs, without which we think we cannot be whole. We talk of 'needing' the approval or acceptance of others, but our true need is to glorify God and love our neighbour.

The answer to the fear of man is the fear of God. We need a bigger vision of God. To fear God is to respect, worship, trust and submit to God. It's the proper response to his glory, holiness, power, love, goodness and wrath. The appearances of God are often described in the Bible in terms of brightness, fire and brilliance. Think of the heat of the sun, with the nuclear reactions within it creating a brilliance that is blinding, even from millions of miles away. Yet there's an intensity and substance to God's glory far beyond that of our sun. God wraps majesty and splendour round him like a cloak (Psalm 93:1). "'To whom will you compare me? Or who is my equal?" says the Holy One' (Isaiah 40:25). The fear of God for Christians no longer involves terror. He's our Father and we come before him with confidence through Christ (Hebrews 4:14–16). But we can never get chummy with him. He remains a consuming fire. 'My flesh trembles in fear of you,' says the psalmist. 'I stand in awe of your laws' (Psalm 119:120).

So, if you're controlled by people's expectations, you need to learn the fear of God, for it can be taught and learned (Deuteronomy 4:10; 17:18–19; 31:12; Psalm 34:9–11). Meditate on God's glory, greatness, holiness, power, splendour, beauty, grace, mercy and love. Often, in Psalms 18 and 34 for example, this is what the psalmist is doing. In the face of some threat, he speaks the truth about God to himself. He reminds himself of God's glory so that fear of others is replaced by trust in God.

---

9 Edward T. Welch, *When People Are Big and God Is Small: Overcoming peer pressure, codependency, and the fear of man* (Phillipsburg, NJ: P&R Publishing, 1997), p. 15.

When you meet someone whom you fear or whose approval you crave, imagine God next to them. Who is the most glorious, majestic, holy, beautiful, threatening, loving? Whose approval really matters to you? 'Do not be afraid of those who kill the body but cannot kill the soul,' says Jesus. 'Rather, be afraid of the One who can destroy both soul and body in hell' (Matthew 10:28).

Fear in the face of threat is natural, but natural fear needs to be regulated by faith in God. Your manager may be a bully but they're not bigger than God. David had good cause to fear others at various points in his life, but he could say:

> The LORD is my light and my salvation –
> whom shall I fear?
> The LORD is the stronghold of my life –
> of whom shall I be afraid?
> (Psalm 27:1–3; see also Psalm 56:3–4)

The fear of God is liberating. We take people's expectations seriously because we want to love them as God commanded. But we're not enslaved by them. We don't serve them for what they can give us in return – approval, affection, security or whatever. By submitting to Christ's lordship, we're truly free to serve others in love (Galatians 5:13).

3 God is good – so we do not have to look elsewhere

I heard the story of an elderly widow in Russia who had taken a job cleaning the stairwells of a grim apartment block. Her state pension covered her own needs, but she wanted to earn extra money for missionaries working in Mongolia. What makes someone do that for people and churches she'll never see in this life? The answer is joy. She's like the man who found treasure in a field 'then in his joy went and sold all he had and bought that field' (Matthew 13:44).

The invitation of the Bible is not to dreary abstinence. It's a call to find in God that which truly satisfies. It's believing that we find lasting fulfilment, satisfaction, joy and identity in knowing God and nowhere else. Whatever sin offers, God offers more, for God offers himself. God isn't just good; he's *better* – better than every-thing else as he is the ultimate source of all true joy.

In John 4, Jesus turns his request for water from a Samaritan woman into an offer of living water: 'Everyone who drinks this water will be thirsty again, but whoever drinks the water I give them will never thirst. Indeed, the water I give them will become in them a spring of water welling up to eternal life' (vv. 13–14). This living water is God himself, communicated to his people through the Holy Spirit (John 7:37–39). Every longing in us is a version of our longing for God. That longing may be a distorted version of our longing for God, but it's still a longing for the God we were made to know. Jonathan Edwards writes:

> God is the highest good of the reasonable creature, and the enjoyment of him is the only happiness with which our souls can be satisfied . . . Fathers and mothers, husbands, wives, children, or the company of earthly friends, are but shadows. But the enjoyment of God is the substance. These are but scattered beams, but God is the sun. These are but streams, but God is the fountain. These are but drops, but God is the ocean.[10]

One of our problems is that we can focus only on the present moment. In it, we think that the pleasures of sin are real and joy in God is insubstantial or distant. But, in truth, it's the other way round: every joy we experience is but a shadow of the source of all joy, which is God himself. Marriage, for example, is a reflec-tion of the joy of union with God; adultery a distorted reflection. If you idolise marriage or commit adultery, then you've settled for less than living water. Sin is like the distorted reflection of a beautiful sunset that shifts with every movement of the breeze across the water. God is the sun itself, in all its beauty, glory and energy.

---

10 Jonathan Edwards, 'The Christian pilgrim: Or, the true Christian's life as a journey towards heaven', in *The Works of Jonathan Edwards* (London: Ball, Arnold & Co., 1840), Vol. 2, p. 244.

That is why nothing but God satisfies – not in a true and lasting way. If you look for satisfaction or fulfilment, meaning or identity anywhere other than in Jesus, you'll be left empty. There may be a moment of refreshment or pleasure, but you'll soon be thirsty again. At the well in John 4, Jesus asks the woman to fetch her husband. It seems like a tangent but, in fact, leads straight to her heart. The truth is, she's had five husbands, and the man she's with now is not her husband. She's been looking for security or fulfilment in marriage, sex or intimacy, but they've been water that's left her thirsty again. No doubt there was pleasure, but it didn't last. It wasn't the real thing. It left her thirsty.

There was a clear pattern to her life. The maths tells the story: five husbands plus another man. What are the patterns in your life? Are the words 'If only . . . ' a refrain you've heard in your life? What comes after the 'If only . . . '? Do you really believe that God is good and lasting satisfaction is to be found in him?

When the Samaritan woman tries to draw Jesus into a first-century version of worship wars, Jesus redefines worship (vv. 19–24). Worship is not about location; it's an attitude of the heart: you worship in spirit and truth. Worship is about what you desire most, what you think has most worth. Every time you look to God to satisfy your longings, you worship him in spirit and in truth. Every time you look elsewhere, you commit idolatry. Even our good works can be idolatrous acts. If we don't delight in God for his own sake, finding him beautiful and glorious in our eyes, then we'll serve him for what we get in return: reputation, security, escape from hell. In so doing, we reveal that our greatest love is our reputation, our security, self-preservation, ourselves.

It's easy for us to think of obedience as the price we pay for entry into heaven. It would be better for us, we suppose, to be living for pleasure but, as Christians, we have to put up with obedience to God. However, the life of obedience is not a bad life or a sad life; it's the *good* life. Life with God and for God is the best life you could live. Remember, change is about *enjoying the freedom from sin and delight in God that God gives to us through Jesus.*

God is not only better than anything sin offers, *God is for ever.* The Bible talks about 'the pleasures of sin' and there's no doubt many sins do bring pleasure. There's no point pretending otherwise. But the Bible also tells us that the pleasures of sin are only for 'a short time'.

> By faith Moses, when he had grown up, refused to be known as the son of Pharaoh's daughter. He chose to be ill-treated along with the people of God rather than to enjoy the fleeting pleasures of sin. He regarded disgrace for the sake of Christ as of greater value than the treasures of Egypt, because he was looking ahead to his reward.
> (Hebrews 11:24–26)

We're called to look beyond the fleeting moment to eternity. 'The wages of sin,' says Paul, 'is death' (Romans 6:23). There is always a price to pay. Often the consequences are in this life – in broken relationships, damaged bodies, a shamed conscience, addictive habits. *Always* there are consequences for the life to come. 'Sin, when it is full-grown,' says James, 'gives birth to death' (James 1:15). We often focus on the temptation. It starts to fill our minds and we lose sight of the bigger picture. One person I know broke a cycle of sin in which they were caught up after visiting a Christian friend dying in a hospice. Suddenly, they were confronted with the bigger picture and forced to look beyond their sin.

Think about Moses. We know from the pyramids and sphinxes that Egyptian rulers were extremely wealthy. This was as good as it got anywhere on earth at that time – the equivalent of today's multimillionaire lifestyles. As a child of the royal court, Moses had it all. But he gave everything up, choosing to be ill-treated with the Hebrew slaves. The reason for this was that he recognised Christ was better than all the treasures of Egypt. The Egyptians locked up their treasures in pyramids to take them into the afterlife, but they couldn't. Instead, their treasures ended up in museums! Moses, however, 'was looking ahead to his reward' (Hebrews 11:26). He realised that what God offered for all eternity was better by far than anything sin could offer in this life.

G. K. Chesterton suggests that, at present, we pursue variety because we're so easily wearied. But what if our 'life and joy were so gigantic that [we] never tired' of routine?

> A child kicks his legs rhythmically through excess, not absence, of life. Because children have abounding vitality, because they are in spirit fierce and free, therefore they want things repeated and unchanged. They always say, 'Do it again' . . . Perhaps God is strong enough to exult in monotony. It is possible that God says every morning, 'Do it again' to the sun; and every evening, 'Do it again' to the moon. It may not be automatic necessity that makes all daisies alike; it may be that God makes every daisy separately, but he has never got tired of making them. It may be that He has the eternal appetite of infancy; for we have sinned and grown old, and our Father is younger than we. The repetition in Nature may not be a mere recurrence; it may be a theatrical encore.[11]

We are so easily bored with life. We are weary with a sin-induced sense of futility. But God is never bored with life. He *is* life. His joy and life are so gigantic that he never tires of sunrises and daisies, of beauty and life and joy. In Proverbs 8:30–31, Jesus, personified as wisdom, speaks of his delight and joy in creation. Jesus says, in effect, 'I was filled with fresh delight day after day, always laughing in his presence, playing in every corner of his world and delighting in humanity.'[12] We worry that eternity will be boring, but that's because we're dead and tired. We look for joy in sin and we're quickly bored, repeatedly moving on in search of more. We're wearied in our futile pursuit of ever-greater excitement. But in eternity, there will be a 'rush to life' running through our veins. Our life and joy will be gigantic, so each moment will bring fresh ecstasy;

---

11 G. K. Chesterton, 'The ethics of Elfland', in *Orthodoxy* (Thirsk: House of Stratus, 2001), p. 41.

12 See Calvin G. Seerveld, *Rainbows for the Fallen World: Aesthetic life and artistic task* (Toronto: Toronto Tuppence Press, 1980), p. 53.

each daisy will be a fresh delight; each sunrise a fresh wonder. We will cry to God, 'Again, again, do it again!' Now we are old and tired and cynical, but then we will be young again – forever young, forever delighting in God.

4 God is gracious – so we do not have to prove ourselves

I lay awake long into the night, replaying the conversation in my mind. The next morning, the brooding continued. Our team meeting had developed into what my daughter later described as 'war'.

Same place, same time, but the night before, a woman in our church had come to me with a profound pastoral crisis. That night I'd slept soundly. How crazy! I could forget a genuine crisis, happy to leave it in God's hands, but an argument about nothing totally preoccupied me. But it was my desire to be vindicated that had consumed me. That's why I'd played my role in creating the conflict in the first place. I wanted to be proved right, so I fought on. What set me free from my self-centred brooding was the truth that God is gracious. I didn't need to justify myself. I couldn't justify myself. But God has graciously justified me through the finished work of Christ. God is 'a forgiving God, gracious and compassionate, slow to anger and abounding in love' (Nehemiah 9:17b).

The parable of the prodigal son in Luke 15 reveals the remarkable grace of God. Asking for your inheritance was tantamount to the younger brother saying, 'I wish you were dead.' Selling off that inheritance was shameful because it meant losing the family's land. Moving to another city was a rejection of his family. And we haven't even got to the wild living! Feeding pigs was as low as you could go for a good Jew because pigs were unclean. Then wanting to eat their food . . . ! This son is a picture of you and me. We've wished God dead, rejected his love and moved as far from him as we can. We've tried to break free from love and ended up in the pigsty, longing to be satisfied by rubbish.

But the gracious behaviour of the father is even more shocking. This would have left Jesus' hearers gasping. If a son asked his father for his inheritance while the father was still alive, the father would disinherit him. If a son tried to break free from his father's rule, the father would beat him. If a son left home to indulge in wild living, the father would disown him. But this father runs to meet his returning son. He doesn't wait for his son to honour him but honours the son with a robe, a ring and a party. This is God – embracing us, welcoming us, honouring us.

I used to think that when I let God down, I would probably have a bad day or my prayers would be unanswered. I assumed that God would act in the way I act when people let me down, giving them the cold shoulder. Or I thought that I could atone by having a miserable day or sweating it out in prayer – as though the death of Jesus hadn't quite done the job. When we think like this, we stand at a distance from God. And all the time he's looking for us, ready to embrace us, ready to welcome us home. Indeed, as the other parables of Luke 15 remind us, it's God who takes the initiative to bring us home (vv. 3–10).

If the story of the younger brother reveals God's grace, in the elder brother we see many characteristics of *not* truly believing that God is gracious.

Restless anger

'The elder brother became angry and refused to go in' (v. 28). He's angry because the younger brother is being honoured as though *he's* in the right. All the elder brother's hard work seems to count for nothing. That's the scandal of God's grace. Without grace, we view life as a contract between us and God: we do good works and, in return, he blesses us. When things go well, we're filled with pride. But when things go badly, either:

- we blame ourselves = feelings of guilt or anger towards ourselves
- we blame God = feelings of bitterness and anger towards God.

Because we often leave God out of our explanations, this anger towards God may be ill-defined. We're not even sure *why* we're angry.

The reality is that the contract or covenant between us and God already reads, 'Paid in full by the blood of Jesus.' Only when we grasp God's grace are we free to serve him for his own sake, not for reward.

Joyless duty

'All these years I've been slaving for you' (v. 29). The elder son doesn't say that he's been 'serving', 'partnering' or 'working' with his father, but 'slaving'. Imagine a woman who cooks for an ungrateful and unkind family. For her, work is drudgery. Now imagine a young bride whose husband is attentive, kind and loving. Whatever she serves up, he thinks it's wonderful because he receives it in love. Does the loved bride find her work drudgery? Of course not. Joyless duty will be what characterises our attitude if we think of God as an uncaring manager. But when we see him as a gracious Father, our attitude will be to offer him our joyful service.

Anxious performance

'[I] never disobeyed your orders' (v. 29). The elder brother wants people to know about his good works because he's trying to prove himself. There are people trying to perform day after day – Christian leaders trying to preach a wonderful sermon every week, parents trying to produce lovely children, workers putting in long hours at work – all in a desperate attempt to prove themselves. Some weeks they feel like they've pulled it off; other weeks it seems so fragile – as though it all might shatter. So they live in a constant state of stress and busyness, always striving to put in another great performance, always worried that the charade might be exposed. The truth is, we can't justify ourselves, but then we don't have to! God is gracious: he throws his arms around us as the father did to the returning prodigal.

Proud comparisons

'This son of yours who has squandered your property with prostitutes' (v. 30). This is the first mention of prostitutes. But the elder brother has assumed this to paint his brother in the worst possible light. We highlight other people's faults so that we look better. Or we disguise pride as kindness and patronise people. We think of right-eousness as a ladder and our position on the ladder is what matters. We feel good about ourselves when we can see people below us, who are less godly, less knowledgeable, less fruitful. But God's grace turns our assessments on their head. We all stand together at the foot of the cross, equally guilty and equally accepted. Jesus tells the parable of the prodigal son because the Pharisees are muttering about him welcoming sinners and eating with them (vv. 1–2). It turns out that the Son of God isn't interested in respectability or self-righteousness; he's interested in repentant sinners. Jesus is right to party with notorious sinners because heaven is a party for sinners (vv. 7, 10, 23–24).

Many of us are confident that we'll be justified on the last day – acquitted before God through the death of Jesus. But what about justification today and tomorrow? Are you still trying to prove yourself?

- Do you ever get angry or brood after an argument because you want to prove you're in the right?
- Does your Christian service feel like joyless duty?
- Do you ever feel the pressure to perform?
- Do you serve others so you can feel good about yourself or impress people?
- Do you look down on others or exaggerate their failings?
- Do you worry that you won't make the grade in life?
- Do you enjoy conversations about the shortcomings of others?

The elder son doesn't see himself as a son at all, but as a slave. The father has his obedience, but not his love. Does God the Father have your obedience, but not your love?

Here's the shocking truth: without justifying faith, people 'never do anything out of love to God, but only out of self-love or fear of damnation'.[13] There are acts that look like good works but, in fact, reflect a belief that the best way to get in God's good books or prove

---

13 The Belgic Confession, article 24.

myself to others is through what I do. In effect, I declare myself to be a better saviour than Jesus. We think that we must finish off what Christ left undone. That's why Jesus says, 'The work of God is this: to believe in the one he has sent' (John 6:29). There's only one thing God wants us to do: have faith in his Son. Everything else will flow from that.

Richard Lovelace claims that the main reason Christians do not change is a failure to really grasp God's grace:

> Christians who are no longer sure that God loves and accepts them in Jesus, apart from their present spiritual achievements, are subconsciously radically insecure persons . . . Their insecurity shows itself in pride, a fierce defensive assertion of their own righteousness and defensive criticism of others.[14]

All is not lost. The father goes out to plead with the elder brother (Luke 15:28). He welcomes his prodigal son and he welcomes his self-righteous son. At the end of the story, the elder brother is still on the outside of the party. We're left wondering what he'll do. It forces us to wonder what *we* would do – what we *will* do. Will we live believing that God is gracious?

In the Temple, the work of atonement was never done. The priests were at it day after day (Hebrews 10:11–12). But Jesus has finished. He's done all that's required. So we can sit down too. We don't have to be up and busy atoning, proving ourselves, earning God's blessing, performing.

> View him prostrate in the garden;
> on the ground your Maker lies;
> then on Calvary's tree behold him,
> hear him cry before he dies:
> 'It is finished! It is finished!'
> Sinner, will not this suffice?[15]

---

14 Richard F. Lovelace, *Dynamics of Spiritual Life: An Evangelical theology of renewal* (Downers Grove, IL: IVP Academic, 1979), pp. 211–12.

15 Joseph Hart, 'Come, ye sinners, poor and wretched', 1759.

Conclusion

We can only sin if we suffer from a radical loss of perspective. Only if we forget that God is great and good can we sin. But that is what we do time after time. We forget our God and the identity he gives us.

Change takes place through faith in our great and good God. It takes place as we preach truth to our hearts. This doesn't mean that it's easy. Jesus says 'just believe' because it's faith and faith alone that makes the difference (Mark 5:36). But that's a big 'just'! Faith is a daily struggle. Lies about God are all around us: the world, the flesh and the devil whisper them continually to our hearts. It's a struggle. But it's also possible: 'This is the victory that has overcome the world, even our faith' (1 John 5:4).

What does this mean in practice? First, we need to nurture our trust in God's greatness, fear of God's glory, delight in God's goodness, longing for God's future and rest in God's grace. We need to do this day by day through the word, prayer and the Christian community (more of this in Chapter 8).

Second, when we face temptation, we need to say not only 'I should not do this' but also *'I need not do this'*. When tempted to envy, we should say not only 'I must not envy' but also 'I *need* not envy because I have Christ.' When tempted to worry, we should say not only 'I must not worry' but also 'I *need* not worry because God is in control.' Whatever sin offers, God is bigger and better. To say to temptation 'I *must* not do this' is legalism. To say 'I *need* not do this because God is bigger and better' is good news.

Reflection #1

What might be the lies behind the following behaviour or emotions? There may well be several possible answers. What truths do each of these people need to turn to in faith?

1 Abdul often complains. He's been ill for years and the doctors aren't really sure what the problem is. It gets him down and it's all he can ever talk about.

2 Colin's tired. So tired, he often loses patience with the children and, last night, when his wife wanted to talk to him, he fell asleep on the sofa. He's working all the overtime he can get. He wants to be a good provider for his family, but it's a struggle meeting the mortgage payments.

3 Cathy is thinking of moving in with her boyfriend. Her Christian friends tell her it's wrong, but they don't appreciate the way Paul makes her feel loved. She felt so empty before Paul came into her life and now she feels kind of complete. Besides, it's easy for them – they're basically married.

4 Jamal spends hours on computer games. It's damaging his relationships with his family. He's not really living up to his responsibilities. Real life is a bit boring. In real life, he's just an ordinary guy, but in the virtual world, he's a hero.

5 Every morning, Elsa feels the tension in her stomach as she sets off for school. Her classmates bad-mouth their teachers and gossip about others. They obsess about the latest fashions and the boys they're going out with. Every now and then, they make fun of Elsa for not joining in. Sometimes she does things that she knows are wrong. Most of the time she just feels on the edge.

6 Carla often gossips about people. She loves to put them down and point out their faults. It makes her feel good about herself.

Reflection #2

Paul Tripp talks about our circles of responsibility and of concern (see Figure 1 and Table 2).[16] The circle of responsibility contains those things that are important to me and which I can influence. Around this is a larger circle – the circle of concern. This contains things that are important to me but which are beyond my ability to change.

Think about your life. What belongs in the circle of responsibility? What belongs in the circle of concern? Do you have anything in the wrong circle? What behaviour is this leading to?

16 Paul David Tripp, *Instruments in the Redeemer's Hands: People in need of change helping people in need of change* (Phillipsburg, NJ: P&R Publishing, 2002), pp. 250–5.

⇨ Putting things that should be in the circle of responsibility into the circle of concern leads to shirking responsibility.
⇨ Putting things that should be in the circle of concern into the circle of responsibility leads to worry or manipulation or overbusyness.

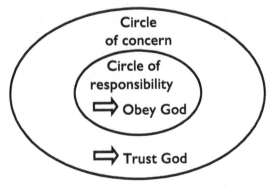

Figure 1 **The circles of responsibility and concern**

Table 2 What the circles of responsibility and concern contain

Circle	Contents	Examples	My duty
Circle of responsibility	Things that are important to me and which I can change	Being a godly spouse, partner, parent, child, friend and church member	To obey God
Circle of concern	Things that are important to me and which I cannot change	Love from a spouse, conversion of a friend, financial security	To trust God

Change project

Question 5: What truths do you need to turn to?

What thoughts are behind your behaviour or emotions?

Think about the issue you've identified for your change project.

- Why do you do what you do or feel?
- What do you hope to achieve?
- What do you think will make you happy in that situation?
- What beliefs or thoughts shape your behaviour or emotions?

What's the lie?

Behind every sin and every negative emotion is a lie. What's the lie behind the issue you've chosen for your change project?

What do your thoughts show about your trust in God?

It's important to express your beliefs or thoughts as beliefs or thoughts about God. We don't always do this. We leave God out of the picture. As a result, we don't see our thoughts as lies about God. So restate your thinking with God included. The following questions may help.

- If you want something, do you think it offers more than God offers?
- If you fear something, do you think that it is more important than God?
- If you're angry about something, do you feel God has let you down?

What truths do you need to turn to?

Turn the answer to your previous question the opposite way round. If this is the lie, what's the truth? Which of the following truths particularly apply to the lies behind the area you've chosen for your change project?

- God is great – so we do not have to be in control.
- God is glorious – so we do not have to fear others.
- God is good – so we do not have to look elsewhere.
- God is gracious – so we do not have to prove ourselves.

The following passages of Scripture talk about these truths. Meditate on them. Turn them into prayer. Ask God to help you to remember them and believe them in moments of temptation.

- God is great – Psalm 27.
- God is glorious – Psalm 31.
- God is good – Psalm 84.
- God is gracious – Psalm 103.

Write a summary of the truths you need to turn to in faith.

6

What desires do you need to turn from?

Therefore, with minds that are alert and fully sober, set your hope on the grace to be brought to you when Jesus Christ is revealed at his coming. As obedient children, do not conform to the evil desires you had when you lived in ignorance. But just as he who called you is holy, so be holy in all you do; for it is written: 'Be holy, because I am holy.'
(1 Peter 1:13–16)

God's agenda for our lives is to be holy, just as he is holy. This holiness is the fruit of what we think or trust and what we desire or worship. We've seen that sinful behaviour arises when we believe lies about God instead of trusting God's word. So Peter tells us to have 'minds that are alert and fully sober' (v. 13). We're to fill our minds with truth and battle our unbelieving thoughts. Peter also tells us not to 'conform to the evil desires' we had when we 'lived in ignorance' (v. 14; see also 1 Peter 2:11). The other thing going on in our hearts is that we desire, worship, love, treasure. We sin because we desire or worship idols instead of worshipping God.

We desire or worship idols

We don't often think of ourselves worshipping idols because we think of them as statues or shrines, but God tells the leaders of Israel that they 'have set up idols in their hearts' (Ezekiel 14:3). We shouldn't look down on the Israelites for worshipping idols; we should instead see a mirror of our own hearts. John Calvin says,

'Man's nature, so to speak, is a perpetual factory of idols.'[1] God says, 'My people have committed two sins: They have forsaken me, the spring of living water, and have dug their own cisterns, broken cisterns that cannot hold water.' As a result, you 'follow other gods to your own harm' and your 'own shame' (Jeremiah 2:13; 7:6, 19). An idol is anything we look to instead of God for living water. Our double sin is, first, to reject the truth of God's greatness and goodness and, second, to place our affections elsewhere.

> God is that in which we are to look for all good and in which we are to find refuge in all need. Therefore . . . anything on which your heart relies and depends, I say, that is really your God.[2]

> Idolatry may not involve explicit denials of God's existence or character. It may well come in the form of an over-attachment to something that is, in itself, perfectly good . . . An idol can be a physical object, a property, a person, an activity, a role, an institution, a hope, an image, an idea, a pleasure, a hero – anything that can substitute for God.[3]

> *Our idols are those things we count on to give our lives meaning.* They are the things of which we say, 'I need this to make me happy,' or 'If I don't have this my life is worthless and meaningless'.[4]

The New Testament's way of talking about idolatry is in terms of our 'sinful desires'. It's literally 'the lusts of the flesh'. 'Lusts' here refers to not just sexual desire but all sinful desire. And 'flesh' is not talking about our bodies but about our old selves, with our bias

---

1   John Calvin, *Institutes of the Christian Religion*, ed. John T. McNeill, trans. Ford Lewis Battles (Philadelphia, PA/London: Westminster/SCM Press, 1961), 1.11.8.

2   Martin Luther on the first commandment in 'The large catechism', in Kirsi I. Stjerna (ed), *The Annotated Luther: Volume 2: Word and faith* (Minneapolis, MN: Fortress Press, 2015), p. 300.

3   Richard Keyes, cited in Os Guinness and John Seel (eds), *No God But God: Breaking with the idols of our age* (Chicago, IL: Moody, 1992), p. 33.

4   Timothy Keller, *Apprenticeship Manual* (Church of the Redeemer), Unit 2.4.

towards the sin we have from birth. Paul describes greed as idolatry (Colossians 3:5). Your idol is whatever you're greedy for. It may be money, approval, sex or power. David Powlison says, 'If "idolatry" is the characteristic and summary Old Testament word for our drift from God, then "desires" is the characteristic and summary New Testament word for the same drift. Both are shorthand for the problem of human beings.'[5] In other words, the sinful desires of the flesh is an alternative expression for the idols of the heart.

Another way of thinking about this is to ask what it is we treasure. 'For where your treasure is,' says Jesus, 'there your heart will be also' (Matthew 6:21). Whatever you treasure most is the thing that has captured your heart and so controls your life. This process is described well by the word 'captivated'. We're made captive by our desires.

We confuse free will with self-willed. We think we're free if we get to do what we want. We think we're free when we break away from God. But we become enslaved by our own selfish desires. 'People are slaves to whatever has mastered them' (2 Peter 2:19). 'No one can serve two masters. Either you will hate the one and love the other, or you will be devoted to the one and despise the other. You cannot serve both God and money' (Matthew 6:24). We serve whatever our hearts desire most. If that desire is for God and his glory, then God is our master. But if, for example, our desire is for money, then money is our master – and that's idolatry. Money has become our 'mammon'.

'When the woman saw that the fruit of the tree was good for food and pleasing to the eye, and also desirable for gaining wisdom, she took some and ate it. She also gave some to her husband, who was with her, and he ate it' (Genesis 3:6). 'Good . . . pleasing . . . desirable'. Elyse Fitzpatrick comments that 'Our choices are predicated upon what we think is "good," what we "delight in," what we find most "desirable." The truth about our choices is that we always choose what we believe to be our best. We always choose what we

5 David Powlison, 'Idols of the heart and "Vanity Fair"', *Journal of Biblical Counselling*, Winter 1995, 13(2), p. 36.

believe will bring us the most delight.'[6] Eve thought that the fruit could give her more than God, so she desired the fruit. That desire controlled her heart and determined her behaviour. Just as this was true of the first sin, it's true of all subsequent sins. 'Each person is tempted when they are dragged away by their own evil desire and enticed. Then, after desire has conceived, it gives birth to sin; and sin, when it is full-grown, gives birth to death' (James 1:14–15). Sin begins with desire. We're not sinners because we commit sinful acts. We commit sinful acts because we're sinners, born with a bias to sin, enslaved by our sinful desires. That's why we can't change ourselves simply by changing our behaviour. We need God to change us, by renewing our hearts and giving us new desires.

Every sin begins in the heart with a sinful desire.

> God gave them over in the sinful desires of their hearts to sexual impurity for the degrading of their bodies with one another. They exchanged the truth of God for a lie, and worshipped and served created things rather than the Creator – who is for ever praised. Amen.
> (Romans 1:24–25)

We've seen how sin arises because we exchange the truth about God for a lie. Now we see that sin also arises because God gives us over to the sinful desires of our hearts. It arises when we worship or desire created things rather than the Creator. So our double problem is that we believe lies rather than believing God (Chapter 5), and worship idols rather than worshipping God (Chapter 6).

Desire is at the helm of our lives. It determines our behaviour. As far as our circumstances allow, *we always do what we want to do*. The question is, which of our desires is strongest at any given moment? An alcoholic may desire or want a drink, but refrain from having one. It *looks* like they're not doing what they want, but what has happened is another desire (perhaps to avoid shame or

---

6 Elyse Fitzpatrick, *Idols of the Heart: Learning to long for God alone* (Phillipsburg, NJ: P&R Publishing, 2001), pp. 80–1.

not lose their family) has 'trumped' the desire for a drink. They're still doing what they want – it's just that the desire for a drink is no longer their biggest desire.[7] We excuse ourselves by thinking that, while we do want to be good, we are the victims of other factors (our circumstances, history, biology, ill health and so on). But the Bible's radical view of sin tells us that we *are* responsible. We always do what we want to do.

But this also gives us hope. In Romans 7, Paul describes someone who says: 'For I do not do the good I want to do, but the evil I do not want to do – this I keep on doing' (v. 19). At first sight, this might seem to contradict what we've be saying. Here is someone who *doesn't* do what they want to do. But the *reason* they don't follow their good desires is that their sinful desires are stronger and, therefore, controlling (1:24–26; 7:23–25). The answer, says Paul, is the Holy Spirit and the new desires he gives:

> Those who live according to the flesh have their minds set on what the flesh desires; but those who live in accordance with the Spirit have their minds set on what the Spirit desires . . . Those who are in the realm of the flesh cannot please God. You, however, are not in the realm of the flesh but are in the realm of the Spirit, if indeed the Spirit of God lives in you. (8:5, 8–9)

This understanding humbles us, but it also gives us hope that we can change. We're changed by faith as we look on the glory of God, finding him more desirable than anything sin might offer. By faith and through the Spirit, the desire for God 'trumps' the desire for sin.

When desires go bad

Desires themselves aren't wrong – they are part of being human. We should, however, desire God and his glory (1 Corinthians 12:31). A sinful desire is one that, for us, is bigger than God. It

---

7 This argument is from Jonathan Edwards, 'The freedom of the will', in *The Works of Jonathan Edwards* (London: Ball, Arnold & Co., 1840), Vol. 1, I.II.

could be a desire for *a good thing, but it has become more important to us than God.* The word translated as 'sinful desires' is 'epithumiai', or, 'overdesires'. To paraphrase Calvin:

> Our problem is not the natural desires God wrote into our character at creation, the desires [for love, order, pleasure] that make us human. Our problem is desires which struggle against God's control . . . Human desires are evil and sinful, not because we desire unnatural things, but because our desires are inordinate.[8]

As we have seen, it's not usually the thing we want that's the problem but the fact that we want it more than God. To want to be married or successful or healthy, for example, is to desire a good thing. But if my singleness or failure or illness makes me bitter, then my desire has grown too big – bigger than my desire for God. As a result, I cannot be content with God's sovereignty over my life.

The world is full of good things given by God. We can and should enjoy them with relish. But they're meant to be bridges to joy in God. We should delight in the gifts *and* the Giver. We do this by receiving them with thanksgiving. 'For everything God created is good, and nothing is to be rejected if it is received with thanksgiving, because it is consecrated by the word of God and prayer' (1 Timothy 4:1–5). Even in this, we need to take care that *a good thing doesn't become a 'god thing'*, eclipsing God, because the gift matters more to us than the Giver.

In John 6, Jesus miraculously feeds five thousand people with just five loaves and two fish. The next day, the crowd come wanting more. Here are people who came to Jesus looking for satisfaction. What could be wrong with that? It's that they're not interested in Jesus himself, they simply want a free meal. 'Jesus answered, "Very truly I tell you, you are looking for me, not because you saw the signs I performed but because you ate the loaves and had your fill"'

---

8 Paraphrased from John Calvin, *Institutes of the Christian Religion*, ed. John T. McNeill, trans. Ford Lewis Battles (Philadelphia, PA/London: Westminster/SCM Press, 1961), 3.3.12.

(v. 26). Jesus urges them not to look to him to realise their idolatrous desires, but to find the true satisfaction that he offers: 'Do not work for food that spoils, but for food that endures to eternal life, which the Son of Man will give you' (v. 27).

These people wanted Jesus to meet their immediate desires. It can be the same with us. We look to God to provide for our material and emotional needs. And often he does. But God always has a bigger agenda. He wants us to know him and serve him. He wants us to become like his Son. When our desires grow more important to us than Jesus, then God will stick to his bigger agenda.

'The heart is deceitful above all things' (Jeremiah 17:9). The lusts of the heart are 'deceitful desires' (Ephesians 4:22). One common way that desires deceive us is by masquerading as 'needs'. We don't say, 'I lust to be loved.' We say, 'I need to be loved.' We take a good desire (to be loved) and turn it into an idolatrous desire and call it a need. God and his glory are no longer at the centre of my outlook. Instead, *I'm* at the centre, demanding that people 'worship' me by giving me affection and affirmation. Richard Lovelace calls it our 'god complex'.[9]

God promises to meet our true needs, but we can't expect him to meet our selfish desires. God isn't a divine waiter, ready to serve up whatever we want. God isn't the key to the good life as I choose to define it. He *is* the good life, he defines it. God must be desired for his own sake, not as the purveyor of worldly success.

Carolyn wanted a husband and was looking to God to provide one. She had tried to live a godly life, but God, she claimed, hadn't kept his side of the bargain, so she was bitter towards him. In the course of several conversations, I spoke of God's grace. But talk of grace didn't bring change to Carolyn's life. What I didn't see at the time was that there was a bigger, more fundamental problem in her heart. Carolyn's desire for a husband had become an idol. She wanted a husband more than she wanted God. So, when God didn't provide her with one, she become bitter towards him. What

---

9 Richard F. Lovelace, *Dynamics of Spiritual Life: An Evangelical theology of renewal* (Downers Grove, IL: IVP Academic, 1979), p. 90.

I should have said to her was, 'Taste and see that the LORD is good' (Psalm 34:8) and 'Turn from your idolatry; find satisfaction in the Bread of Life and you will never be hungry.'

Through the prophet Amos, God speaks of a gift that he gave to his people: 'empty stomachs' (v. 4:6). He 'withheld rain' so that 'people staggered from town to town for water' (vv. 7–8). He struck their crops with blight and mildew (v. 9). These might seem strange gifts, but God gave them so that his people might repent. Empty stomachs are terrible things, but idolatry and its consequences are worse. God always seeks the best for his people, and that best is himself. Famine and thirst are acts of divine love when their aim is to bring us back to God.

Repentance: turning from our sinful desires

As we have seen, sin arises because we desire something more than we desire God. Overcoming sin begins by reversing this process: desiring God more than other things. The Bible calls this 'repentance'. The word means 'turning': we turn away from our idolatrous desires and turn in faith towards God.

Fundamentally, sin is an orientation towards ourself. We won't let God be God of our lives. We run our lives *our* way, without him. 'Self' is at the centre of the picture. Repentance is a reorientating of ourselves back towards God. It's putting God at the centre. What matters most is no longer our pleasure or success, or even our problems, but God's glory (2 Corinthians 12:7–9).

Yet, instinctively we think of ourselves as at the centre of our world. We think of our life as a story and, if we're Christians, God is one of the characters in our story. We look for him when we need him; expect him to be grateful when we serve him. He's a delightful part of our story, but we think of it as *our* story. But it's not our story, it's *God*'s story. Of course, God is there for us – he graciously comes to our aid when we're in need. But the bigger reality is that we're there for God. We exist to give him glory. He doesn't owe us anything – not even explanations. Meanwhile, we owe him everything, as our Creator and Redeemer. And it's so much better to be a minor character in God's story than to try to write our own script.

Living with God at the centre is the good and sane life. It's better to enjoy the warmth of the sun than light a bonfire in your home. It's better to reflect the glory of God than to be consumed with the empty pursuit of our own glory.

One of my recurrent sins is self-pity. If someone treats me badly, I get in a huff. If something goes wrong, I'm grumpy. Sometimes I just wake up in a black mood. I act as though *I'm* what matters in my life; like I'm the axis on which my world spins. But I'm not. I was made to glorify God and enjoy him for ever. I may need to give myself a stiff talking to, but there's such freedom in accepting that this is God's world and not mine. I'm grumpy because things aren't going my way, but I've no right and no need to expect them to go my way. It's enough to know that they're going God's way and his ways are good.

This new God-centred perspective is both humbling and liberating. It's humbling because it puts us in our place. We're not the centre of the world. We're not even the centre of *our* world. But it's also liberating. We no longer need to try continually to be in control. We can let God be God. Our reputation is no longer what matters. We're no longer controlled by the approval or rejection of others. We're free to serve others in love.

Continual repentance

We become Christians through faith and repentance, and we grow as Christians through continual faith and repentance. We don't graduate from the gospel to some advanced way of holiness or progress. Martin Luther said, 'To progress is always to begin again.'[10]

So repentance is not a one-off event that only takes place at our conversion. John Calvin says, 'God assigns to [Christians] a race of repentance, which they are to run throughout their lives.'[11] Repentance is a lifelong, continual activity of turning back to God from God-dethroning desires. And repentance is not just turning

---

10 Martin Luther, *Lectures on Romans*, Library of Christian Classics, Vol. 15, ed. and trans. Wilhelm Pauck (Philadelphia, PA/London: Westminster/SCM Press, 1961), p. 128.

11 John Calvin, *Institutes of the Christian Religion*, ed. John T. McNeill, trans. Ford Lewis Battles (Philadelphia, PA/London: Westminster/SCM Press, 1961), 3.3.9.

from sinful behaviour but also turning from the idols and desires that cause sinful behaviour.

One way in which the Bible describes the ongoing activity of repentance is 'mortification'. It means putting sin to death: 'Put to death, therefore, whatever belongs to your earthly nature: sexual immorality, impurity, lust, evil desires and greed, which is idolatry' (Colossians 3:5). It means continually saying a decisive 'No' to sin in our lives, especially at the earliest stages of temptation.

Sin is mortified in our lives *through Christ* and *by the Spirit*. The foundation of mortification is Christ's work on the cross: 'For we know that our old self was crucified with [Christ] so that the body ruled by sin might be done away with, that we should no longer be slaves to sin' (Romans 6:6; see also Galatians 2:20; 5:24). Christ dealt a fatal blow to our self under sin at the cross, freeing us from its power. It's because we 'died with Christ' and 'have been raised with Christ' that we're to 'put to death, therefore, whatever belongs to your earthly nature' (Colossians 2:20; 3:1, 5). We do this in the power of the Spirit: 'if by the Spirit you put to death the misdeeds of the body, you will live' (Romans 8:13). The Spirit gives a new heart with new God-glorifying desires. Repentance (turning from sinful desires) or mortification (killing off sinful desires) is Christ's work for us and the Spirit's work in us. But, with the Spirit's help, we are active participants in the process.

Mortification is like gardening. We need to weed out the sins in our lives. My garden is plagued by different kinds of weeds. We've inherited some tree stumps. Shifting them is hard work – you need a pickaxe, a whole afternoon and my friend Steve. We also have a lot of scarlet pimpernel. That's easy to dig up, but neglect it a few weeks and it will quickly take over. We've also got brambles. You can pull them easily enough, provided you wear thick gloves, but if you leave even a small piece of root in the ground, they'll come again.

Sometimes weeding out sin is like pulling up tree stumps. A particular sin may have gripped our heart for so long that its roots run deep. It's become a habit. Pulling it up will be hard and painful work, like removing a tree stump. It's better by far to pull up any weeds of sin as soon as they emerge, when they're still small and rootless, like the scarlet pimpernel. But this is a continual task. Every day we neglect to do it makes the job harder. The key thing is to mortify the roots of sin. We need to be putting sinful desires to death, not just changing behaviour. Otherwise, sin will be like my brambles, growing again from any piece of root left behind. Of course, I don't know where bramble roots are until they emerge from the ground, but when I see the shoots, I can dig out the roots. When you see sinful behaviour, follow it back to its root. Sinclair Ferguson says:

> What then is this killing of sin? It is the constant battle against sin which we fight daily – the refusal to allow the eye to wander, the mind to contemplate, the affections to run after anything which will draw us from Christ. It is the deliberate rejection of any sinful thought, suggestion, desire, aspiration, deed, circumstance or provocation at the moment we become conscious of its existence.[12]

'At the moment we become conscious of its existence.' My problem is that I don't do this. A sinful desire gives rise to temptation and I think, 'I'm not actually sinning.' So I play with the thought in my mind. I let my eyes linger. I let my mind wander. And so the desire grows. I feed it and encourage it, and then complain that it's too strong. And all the time I *am* sinning – maybe not in my actions, but in my will because I've not said 'No' to sin.[13] We need to discipline our hearts to say 'No' the *moment* we become conscious of sinful desires.

I've found so much freedom simply by realising that sinful desires are sinful.

- I feel myself getting bitter. Once I might have fed my desires by reflecting on all the wrongs I endure. But I realise now that

---

12 Sinclair B. Ferguson, *The Christian Life: A doctrinal introduction* (Edinburgh: Banner of Truth, 1989), p. 162.

13 See John Calvin, *Institutes of the Christian Religion*, ed. John T. McNeill, trans. Ford Lewis Battles (Philadelphia, PA/London: Westminster/SCM Press, 1961), 3.10.10.

bitterness is grumbling against God's goodness. So (in my best moments and with God's help) I try to stop it before it grows.

- I feel myself getting annoyed. Once I might have fed my desires by reflecting on other people's incompetence. But now I realise that I get annoyed because of my desire to be in control instead of trusting God's sovereignty. And so I try to stop before it grows.
- I feel myself getting angry. Once I might have fed my desires by reflecting on how I've been mistreated. But I realise now that I get angry because of my desire to justify myself instead of trusting in Christ's atoning work. So I try to stop.

It's not necessarily wise to go on an idol hunt all the time or explore every motive. That might lead to an unhealthy introspection. Our focus should be on God's liberating truth. A good guide is to explore your sinful desires only when you see the bad fruit of sinful behaviour and negative emotions in your life. People often ask me, 'How can I tell whether a desire is sinful or not? How can I know whether I desire something too much?' I answer by pointing to Jesus' image of bad fruit growing from a bad tree (Luke 6:43–45). You discover a desire is sinful when it produces bad fruit in your life (disobedience, anger, anxiety and so on). When you see that bad fruit, trace it back to the idolatrous desires of your heart.

Introspective self-analysis is a relatively recent cultural phenomenon. Our Evangelical forebears did self-examination, but it was different. They assumed a clear link between actions and the heart. Spotting that link was made difficult by the deceitfulness of sin, but the answer was not deep introspection. Rather, it was illumination brought by the Spirit and the word. But we live post Freud. Sigmund Freud said that the roots of our actions and emotions are deep in our subconscious. *Because* it's subconscious, we need to dig it out through deep and endless introspection. We often bring this model to sanctification. We think that we need some form of analysis or counselling to undercover the hidden depths of our actions. There may sometimes be some value in this, but our number one need is to look to Christ. 'We cross the line from self-examination to introspection when, in a sense, we do nothing but examine ourselves,' says Martyn Lloyd-Jones. 'If we are always talking to people about ourselves and our problems . . . it probably means that we are all the time centred upon ourselves.'[14] Introspection assumes that I'm what matters in sanctification. But it's God who changes us. Ask God to expose your heart by Spirit through his word (Psalm 139:23–24; Hebrews 4:12–13). But don't linger when looking at yourself. Linger when looking at Christ. As Robert Murray M'Cheyne famously said, 'For one look at yourself, take ten looks at Christ.'[15]

Along with weeding out sin, we need to 'plant in grace'. When other plants are thriving, weeds grow poorly because they're deprived of space, light, water and nutrients. It's the same with Christians. When our thoughts are filled with the glory of God and our lives with the service of God, there'll be less room for sin and temptation (Galatians 6:7–10). We'll come back to this in Chapter 8.

Creating habits, building character

We can sometimes think that small concessions to temptation don't really matter: the lustful look, resentful thoughts, brief fantasy. 'They don't lead to anything,' we tell ourselves. But small concessions don't satisfy temptation – *they fuel it!* Giving in to temptation makes temptation come more frequently and more strongly next time. Sin can become a habit. But turning from sin can also become a habit. Instead of temptation coming more frequently and more strongly, it comes less often and less strongly. In moments of pressure, our minds go to God instead of to sin.

To cross a moral boundary for the first time is hard. Our conscience screams at us to stop. The red lights are flashing and the alarm bells are ringing. But the more frequently you cross that boundary, the easier it becomes to do it. The more you ignore your conscience, the less you notice its warnings. Temptation becomes

---

14 D. Martyn Lloyd-Jones, *Spiritual Depression: Its causes and cure* (London: Pickering & Inglis, 1965), p. 17.

15 Andrew Bonar, *Memoir and Remains of Robert Murray M'Cheyne* (Edinburgh: Banner of Truth, 1966), p. 279.

sin and sin becomes habit. The good news is, we can rebuild the boundary walls. Every time you say 'No' to temptation, you are putting another stone back in the wall. Sinful habits can be replaced by godly character. So tell yourself that the grass on the other side of the moral boundary fence is not greener. It's a place where people are hurt and God is dishonoured. Meanwhile, the grass on this side is good pasture (Psalm 23:1–2; John 10:9–10).

Most of our moral decisions are reflex responses. We act in the moment. Before we know it, malicious words are out of our mouths and we can't take them back. What counts in those situations isn't our ability to do some moral reasoning or biblical reflection. It's the habit of holiness. It's Christian character. It's an undivided heart. Victorian novelist Charles Reade said, 'Sow an act, and you reap a habit. Sow a habit, and you reap a character. Sow a character, and you reap a destiny.'[16]

In 1569, Dirk Willems escaped from a Dutch prison. He was there because he was an Anabaptist – a member of a sect which held that only believing adults should be baptised. Willems fled across a frozen lake, pursued by a prison guard. Half-starved by prison rations, Willems crossed the lake safely, but the guard fell through the ice into the freezing water. Willems immediately turned back and pulled him out. The guard wanted to release Willems, but by then a burgomaster had arrived on the scene. Willems was arrested, tortured and burned at the stake. Willems didn't have time to decide what was the right thing to do. - he reacted in a moment. That's a sign of Christian character. It's a sign that grace has become a habit. You can't create Christian character overnight. It's the fruit of suffering and perseverance (Romans 5:3–4). It's the harvest of the daily weeding out of sin and planting in of grace. Paul Toews comments:

> For Mennonites no other story out of the sixteenth century has so captured the imagination. What Dirk did on that icy pond was reflexive – he didn't have to stop and think whether

---

16 Charles Reade, cited in *The Oxford Dictionary of Quotations* (London: OUP, 1954), p. 406.

it was right or wrong or what the consequences would be. He simply did what his faith compelled him to do. Willems' spontaneous response to someone in need comes only from a heart undivided.[17]

We repent through faith

How do we repent? We repent through faith. We turn back to the worship of God when we believe that God is better than our idols.

In the past, I've sometimes suspected that repentance was an add-on. We're not really saved by faith alone, but faith *plus repentance*. But this isn't true. Turning to God in faith and turning from sin in repentance are the same movement. Try it now. Stand facing towards the window. Then turn to face the opposite wall. The act of turning away from the window and the act of turning towards the wall are one movement. You can't turn towards the wall without turning away from the window. And you can't turn to God in faith without turning away from sin in repentance. When we trust God, we're affirming that he's bigger and better than our sinful desires. Repentance is itself an act of faith.

1 God is bigger than my sinful desires

Sometimes, the pressure of temptation makes us feel that sin is inevitable. A friend once emailed me, 'Temptation comes in two forms: (1) sin seems attractive; (2) sin seems inevitable. We feel like we can't do anything about it. We feel trapped. And so we give in to sin.' That's certainly true of my experience. I say 'No' to temptation, but the temptation keeps coming back. In the end, it no longer seems a question of *whether* I'll give in but *when*. But *this is a lie*. Sin is *not* inevitable for a child of God. We've been set free from its control. I need to believe the truth that God is bigger than my sinful desires. I need faith in God's power if I'm to repent my sin.

---

17 Paul Toews, 'Dirk Willems: A heart undivided', *Profiles of Mennonite Faith*, Fall 1997, No. 1.

2 God is better than my sinful desires

We choose to follow our sinful desires because, in that moment, we believe they offer more than God. Faith is the realisation that God is much, much better than my sinful desires. And when we affirm this in our hearts, we'll inevitably turn away from those deceptive and empty desires to find true satisfaction in God.

Why spend money on what is not bread,
and your labour on what does not satisfy?
Listen, listen to me, and eat what is good,
and you will delight in the richest of fare.'
(Isaiah 55:2)

'O Israel, stay away from idols!
I am the one who answers your prayers and cares for you.
I am like a tree that is always green;
all your fruit comes from me.'
(Hosea 14:8, NLT)

Reflection #1

People tend to think of sins in the plural as consciously willed acts where one was aware of and chose not to do the righteous alternative . . . But God's descriptions of sin often highlight the unconscious aspect. Sin – the desires we pursue, the beliefs we hold, the habits we obey as second nature – is intrinsically deceitful. If we knew we were deceived, we would not be deceived. But we are deceived, unless awakened through God's truth and Spirit. Sin is a darkened mind, drunkenness, animal-like instinct and compulsion, madness, slavery, ignorance, stupor. People often think that to define sin as unconscious removes human responsibility. How can we be culpable for what we did not sit down and choose to do? But the Bible takes the opposite track. The unconscious and semi-conscious nature of much sin simply testifies to the fact that we are steeped in it. Sinners think, want, and act sin-like by nature, nurture, and practice.[18]

Reflection #2

Write a version of Psalm 27 in which you make it say the *opposite* of what it actually says. Here is an example.

The LORD is my light and my salvation – whom shall I fear?	My spouse lights up my life – I crave her approval.
The LORD is the stronghold of my life – of whom shall I be afraid?	My manager guarantees my security – I'm afraid of upsetting them.
When the wicked advance against me to devour me, it is my enemies and my foes who will stumble and fall.	When my peers turn against me, when they mock me, I stumble and fall.

How much of your opposite version reflects the way you really think at times? What are the corresponding truths from the real version of the psalm that counter this wrong thinking about God?

Repeat this exercise with Psalms 31, 84 and 103.

Change project

Question 6: What desires do you need to turn from?

What are the idols of your heart?

- When you're *angry*, what are you not getting that you want?
- When you're *anxious*, what is threatened?

---

18 David Powlison, 'Cure of souls (and the modern psychotherapies)', *Journal of Biblical Counselling*, Spring 2007, 25(2), pp. 25–6.

- When you're *despondent*, what have you lost or failed at?
- What do you think you need to have?
- 'I'd be happy if only I could have . . .'

What are the desires that control your heart?

Revisit the questions relating to Question 4 in Chapter 4. Think about what is going on in your heart when you do or feel the area you've chosen for your change project.

- What did you want, desire or wish for?
- What did you fear? What were you worrying about?
- What did you think you needed?
- What were your strategies and intentions designed to accomplish?
- What or whom were you trusting?
- Whom were you trying to please? Whose opinion of you counted?
- What were you loving? What were you hating?
- What would have you brought you the greatest happiness, pleasure or delight? What would have brought you the greatest pain and misery?[19]

Write a summary of the heart desires from which you need to turn.

---

19 From Elyse Fitzpatrick, *Idols of the Heart: Learning to long for God alone* (Phillipsburg, NJ: P&R Publishing, 2001), p.163.

7

What stops you changing?

'I've tried changing, but I don't seem to get very far.' 'It's the same old story with the same old sin.' 'I could write the manual on holiness, but I still keep falling.' 'I've been working on my change project, but this week has put me back to square one.' We've seen God is at work changing us. So why don't we change more than we do? What stops us changing?

The more I've reflected on my own struggles, on my experience as a pastor and on the Bible, the more I'm persuaded that it comes down to one of two things: a love of self or a love of sin. It's not lack of discipline or knowledge or support. These all matter, but the number one reason people don't change is pride, closely followed by hating the consequences of sin but actually still loving the sin itself. So here are five mindsets that stop us changing:

1 I think I can overcome my sin on my own
2 I don't really think my sin is my fault
3 I don't really think my sin is a big problem
4 It's better to pretend that everything is OK
5 I hate the consequences of my sin but not the sin itself.

1 I think I can overcome my sin on my own

Have you ever been frustrated or angry at your lack of change? Many people have said to me at some point, 'I can't believe I've done it again' or 'I'm so cross with myself for doing this.' I've thought it many times myself, but listen to Ed Welch:

Perhaps the person is mad at himself for repeating the same sin over and over again. This is actually a veiled form of pride that assumes he is capable of doing good in his own power. He is minimizing his spiritual inability apart from God's grace.[1]

Jerry Bridges claims that 'God wants us to walk in obedience – not victory.' Our problem, he explains, 'is that our attitude towards sin is more self-centred than God-centred. We are more concerned about our own "victory" over sin than we are about the fact that our sins grieve the heart of God.'[2]

Pride isn't just a sin; it's part of the definition of sin. Pride puts us in place of God. We turn from our chief end of glorifying God and, instead, make our chief end glorifying ourselves. And we can even do this with sanctification. We make sanctification our achievement and glory. C. J. Mahaney calls it 'cosmic plagiarism.'[3]

This is why humility is a paradigm of repentance. To humble ourselves before God is to repent our god complex. It is why to walk humbly with our God is what God requires (Micah 6:8). 'Scripture says: "God opposes the proud but shows favour to the humble" . . . Humble yourselves before the Lord, and he will lift you up' (James 4:6, 10; 1 Peter 5:5). Humility is the secret to receiving grace. As Jack Miller says, 'grace flows downhill.'[4] People used to talk about the higher life of sanctification, but what we really need is the lower life. 'We grow *up* into Christ by growing *down* into lowliness,' says J. I. Packer.[5] If we truly want the grace of holiness, we must get lower. So humble yourself and leave the lifting up to God.

Humility, of course, isn't some spiritual achievement that merits God's grace. Quite the opposite. It's the realisation that we can never *merit* any blessing from God. It's the recognition that grace is our only hope. It's giving up on ourselves and finding all we need in Jesus.

---

1 Edward T. Welch, *Addictions: A banquet in the grave* (Phillipsburg, NJ: P&R Publishing, 2001), p. 170.

2 Jerry Bridges, *The Pursuit of Holiness* (Colorado Springs, CO: NavPress, 1978), pp. 20–1.

3 C. J. Mahaney, *Humility: True greatness* (Colorado Springs, CO: Multnomah, 2005), p. 80.

4 C. Jack Miller, *The Heart of a Servant Leader: Letters from Jack Miller*, ed. Barbara Miller Juliani (Phillipsburg, NJ: P&R Publishing, 2004), p. 267.

5 J. I. Packer, *A Passion for Holiness* (Wheaton, IL: Crossway, 1992), p. 120.

If you're frustrated at your inability to change, then your first step is to give up – to give up on yourself. Repent your self-reliance and self-confidence. Your second step is to rejoice in God's grace – his grace to forgive and his grace to transform.

2 I don't really think my sin is my fault

We don't like to think of ourselves as bad people. We don't want to think of our hearts as evil. So we don't take responsibility for our sin. We may admit that we need to change, but we don't want to admit that *we* are the problem. And so we have a number of avoidance strategies. Self-reliance says, 'I will do OK by myself.' Self-justification says, 'I'm already doing OK by myself.' Making that claim involves excusing, minimising or hiding sin.

The first sin began with doubting God's word and desiring created things more than the Creator. As we've seen, these are characteristics of all subsequent sin. But another feature of that first sin is a common characteristic of subsequent sin: making excuses. Adam blamed Eve. Eve blamed the serpent (Genesis 3:11–13). And today we still try to pass on the blame for our sin. It's a way to evade taking responsibility for our actions.

We might blame other people for what they've done. 'They provoked me . . . they wound me up . . . they started it . . . I was afraid of what they would say . . . ' Or we might blame other people for what they *haven't* done. 'If you'd helped me more . . . if you'd been there for me . . . if you'd loved me better.'

Or we blame our circumstances: our context, upbringing, personal history or biology (our genes, our chemistry or mood). Consider what this might sound like for someone who gets angry.

- **Context** 'He just made me so mad. It was so unfair. You'd have done the same if you'd been in my situation.'
- **Upbringing**. 'I take after my father. He used to get angry. I learned my anger from him.'
- **Personal history**. 'You'd be an angry person if you'd been through what I've been through.'

- **Biology** 'It's just the way I am. I'm hot-headed. There's nothing I can do about it.'

It's important to acknowledge that there's some truth to all these explanations. These things also reinforce and trigger sin. They often shape the form it takes. But these factors, on their own, do not offer a full explanation for our sin. We choose how we respond to circumstances and it is the thoughts and desires of our heart that determine the choices we make.

Our sinful hearts portray our actions as inevitable, unavoidable or appropriate. If someone lets me down, I assume that my anger is inevitable, unavoidable and appropriate. But the truth is, my anger reveals my idolatrous desires. Jerry Bridges says that we should use the language of disobedience to describe sin rather than defeat:

> When I say I am defeated by some sin, I am unconsciously slipping out from under my responsibility. I am saying something outside of me has defeated me. But when I say I am disobedient, that places the responsibility for my sin squarely on me. We may, in fact, be defeated, but the reason we are defeated is because we have chosen to disobey.[6]

The effect of this is that all our blaming ends up at God's doorstep. We point to other people, our circumstances or our biology. But what we're saying is that it's God's fault. He allowed these circumstances. He made me the way I am. But James says, 'When tempted, no one should say, "God is tempting me." For God cannot be tempted by evil, nor does he tempt anyone; but each person is tempted when they are dragged away by their own evil desire and enticed' (James 1:13–14). God isn't out to get us. Nor does he put us in impossible situations in which we're bound to sin. It's our own evil desires that entice us. 'It's different for me,' we say. 'My circumstances are unique. Other people have choices, but my behaviour's inevitable, so it's not really my fault.' We want to be

---

6 Jerry Bridges, *The Pursuit of Holiness* (Colorado Springs, CO: NavPress, 1978), p. 84.

special – even in our sin! But God says, 'The temptations in your life are no different from what others experience,' and our behaviour is not inevitable: 'And God is faithful. He will not allow the temptation to be more than you can stand. When you are tempted, he will show you a way out so that you can endure' (1 Corinthians 10:13, NLT).

Dorothy and Naomi were two elderly women in my church. Both struggled with the effects of physical pain. Dorothy had a problem with her legs. When you met her she would regale you with her medical problems. It got her down and made her gloomy. Her conversation had one theme: herself.

Naomi had acute arthritis for many years, her fingers curled round into fists. In the last months of her life, cancer ate away at her body. She was in constant physical pain, often wincing. Yet her eyes always shone brightly, and in conversation she spoke of God's goodness and asked after other people.

Both women faced similar circumstances, but if you asked Dorothy what was getting her down, she would say that it was her ailments. Naomi responded to her circumstances in a very different way: the joy of the Lord was her strength.

3 I don't really think my sin is a big problem

Another way we avoid responsibility for sin is by minimising it. We minimise the offence: 'It's not that bad,' 'It was only a small thing.' Or we compare ourselves to others: 'At least I'm not like them,' 'Do you know what they did?' We highlight our goodness: 'Overall, I'm not too bad,' 'I often help others'. These are all things people have said to me. We call sin a 'misdemeanour', 'lapse', 'slip' or 'fall'. We say, I was 'naughty', 'a bit wild', 'thoughtless', 'giddy', 'defeated', 'mischievous', 'clumsy with my words', 'preoccupied', 'ill-disciplined'. We tell 'little white lies' and have 'minor indiscretions'. We have a whole vocabulary to avoid naming sin as sin and evil as evil. 'It was only a little sin,' we say. 'Everyone does it.' 'More a personality trait than a sin.' But sin is serious – so serious, it demands eternal hell or the death of God's eternal Son. True repentance grieves over sin; it never minimises it.

When did you last tremble at God's word? 'These are the ones I look on with favour,' declares the Lord, 'those who are humble and contrite in spirit, and tremble at my word' (Isaiah 66:2). The humble tremble at God's word. They don't minimise sin; they tremble before God. But pride makes us deaf to God's word. We know it already, we suppose, so we don't come to it hungry. We don't engage as needy sinners. Or else our pride suppresses any conviction it might bring because that would shatter our self-esteem.

'It's not my fault. It's not a big deal. Overall, I'm a good person.' These are the ways in which people avoid taking responsibility for their sin. Our response needs to be: 'It *is* your fault. It *is* a big deal. You *are* a bad person.'

Increasingly in our culture, self-fulfilment has become the accepted priority. 'My duty is to myself,' people claim, 'to be the person I want to be or to accept the person I am.' So any talk of guilt is seen as an attack on 'project me'. As a result, even when you highlight my guilt, I'm still the victim because you've just made me feel bad about myself.

I have no desire to make people feel bad about themselves. I want people to know the joy of forgiveness and freedom. But people reject this joy *because* they won't admit that they need our Saviour. We're not victimising ourselves when we talk about sin. We're stepping on to the road of forgiveness and freedom. We find forgiveness and freedom from sin when we repent our sin and turn to God in faith. There's no forgiveness and no freedom without repentance.

And there's no repentance without responsibility. We're *not* repenting when we pass the blame or minimise our sin. There can be no 'buts' in repentance. We can't say, 'I repent my sin, but it's not really my fault.' We can't say: 'I repent my sin, but it wasn't really that bad.' I write these words with deep sorrow because I can think of the people I've known who wouldn't take responsibility for their sin. Including me. In every case it was a tragedy. Some I think were Christians who remained trapped in their sin. Some were people of other faiths or none who will die without God because they won't admit their sin.

There's an episode of *The Simpsons* in which Homer and Bart drift out to sea in a dinghy.[7] Homer wastes their water washing his socks and eats all their rations. When a rescue plane flies overhead, Homer fires a flare, but hits the plane. At one point, as they find themselves in thick fog, Homer is in a hysterical panic, crying out that they're doomed. Then the fog clears and a boat drifts into view. Someone on the boat asks if they're OK, but Homer behaves like a stereotypical man and won't admit his need. He answers that they're fine. The fog closes in again and the boat disappears. And Homer returns to panicking. We can all be like this! We're in desperate straits. We can't rescue ourselves from sin. It fills our lives with tragedy. But when God offers his help, we won't admit our need. We'd rather reject his help than acknowledge our sin.

4 It's better to pretend that everything is OK

One of the main ways in which pride wrecks the process of change is that we hide our sin from others because of it. The problem with this is, 'Whoever conceals their sins does not prosper, but the one who confesses and renounces them finds mercy' (Proverbs 28:13).

We want our good reputation. So we hide, we pretend, we don't seek help. It meshes with proud self-reliance. We want to avoid exposure, so we tell ourselves that we can manage on our own. But here's what's really happening: we are loving our reputation more than we are hating our sin. We'd like to stop sinning, but not if that costs us people's approval. And that means true repentance isn't taking place: 'It is one thing to make a resolution; it is something completely different to repent, diligently seek counsel, and, in concert with others, develop a plan that is concrete and Christ-centred.'[8] Think about it: we're prepared to choose sin, reject God, abandon freedom and even risk hell rather than have people think badly of us.

---

7 *The Simpsons*, 'Boy-Scoutz 'n the Hood', written by Dan McGrath, directed by Jeffrey Lynch (18 November 1993).

8 Edward Welch, 'Self-control: The battle against "one more"', *Journal of Biblical Counselling*, Winter 2001, 19(2), pp. 24–31.

True repentance lets nothing get in the way of change – not even reputation. Are you confessing your sin to a trusted Christian? Are you going to them for accountability? Have you told those who are affected by your sin (your partner or spouse perhaps)? It's not always appropriate to tell a wide circle of people, but you should freely and willingly confess to those to whom you're accountable. You've not done this yet? You're reluctant? Then your reputation still matters more to you than your holiness. Sometimes people continue to feel guilty when God has forgiven them. It's a sign that their opinion ('I am guilty') matters more to them than God's opinion ('You are forgiven')! But people can also continue to feel shame when God has forgiven them. And that's a sign that the opinion of *other people* is what matters most to them. And so you hide your true self. But true repentance is making God central and accepting his declaration that you're righteous in Christ.

Sin is like mould: it grows best in the dark. Expose it to the light and it starts to dry up.

> Everyone who does evil hates the light and will not come into the light for fear that their deeds will be exposed. But whoever lives by the truth comes into the light, so that it may be seen plainly that what they have done has been done in the sight of God.
> (John 3:20–21)

We need to bring our sin into the light.

I once called round to see a new Christian. When I rang the doorbell, no one answered, but I could see the curtains twitching and heard the sound of footsteps. My friend had got drunk again and blown his wages. Now he was hiding (badly) for fear of being exposed. We can all be like my friend (even if some of us are better at it). His hiding is a picture of the way the fear of exposure works. We hide away in the dark with the curtains closed, as it were. We keep our sin secret. But hiding cuts us off from help. We choose darkness instead of light. But hiding leads to sin, and sin leads to hiding. But grace breaks the cycle. Grace disarms the fear of exposure, so allows us to come into the light – into the arena of change.

> We can call sin exactly what it is, regardless of how ugly and shameful it may be, because we know that Jesus bore that sin in His body on the cross. With the assurance of total forgiveness through Christ, we have no reason to hide from our sins anymore.[9]

I want to be known for my holiness, but that desire impedes me actually becoming holy. My pride makes holiness my boast and that cuts me off from my only hope – the grace of God (James 4:6). My pride hides my sin and that cuts me off from the help of other Christians. My pride minimises or excuses sin, so I never deal with it properly. Every day I struggle with the pull between the desire to be known as holy and the desire actually to be holy. The truth I need to keep telling myself is that my reputation is a small price to pay for the joy of knowing more of God and reflecting his glory. I can imagine myself being admired by the crowd or I can imagine myself with God. Being with God seems the far better option. But when I'm among the crowd, the struggle begins again.

5 I hate the consequences of my sin but not the sin itself

We often don't change because we don't really want to. You may react against this. 'I've been struggling with sin for years,' you may say. 'For years I've wanted to be free from it, and now you tell me that I don't really want to?'

But the truth is, we often want to change the *consequences* of sin but *not the sin itself*. We want to do something about the guilt, the fear, the damaged relationships. These outcomes can be a strong motive for seeking help, but in our heart of hearts we still desire the sin itself. In moments of temptation you still think that it offers

---

9 Jerry Bridges, *The Discipline of Grace: God's role and our role in the pursuit of holiness* (Colorado Springs, CO: NavPress, 1994), pp. 22–3.

more than God. I often see this in people's lives. People ask me, as a pastor, to help them sort out the mess of their lives, but they don't really want to change the behaviour that's creating the mess. People want help with debt, but they don't want to change the idolatry of shopping that creates the damaging spending habits. They want help with broken relationships, but they don't want to change the idolatry of self that creates the friction. Imagine that you could commit a sin without any consequences – no one would think worse of you and no judgement would come from God. Would you do it? Answering 'Yes', suggests John Owen, is not really very different from actually sinning. The implication is that we still love the sin more than God. The only thing stopping us is that we fear its consequences more than we love the sin itself. But, says Owen:

> [T]hose who belong to Christ, and whose obedience is shaped by gospel principles, have the death of Christ, the love of God, the detestable nature of sin, the preciousness of communion with God, a deep-seated horror of sin *as sin*, to oppose to all the seductions of sin.[10]

The answer is always the same: faith and repentance. We need to dig deeper to expose the lies in our hearts and repent the idols in our hearts. The New Testament language of repentance is often violent.

- **Amputating** 'If your right eye causes you to stumble, gouge it out and throw it away. It is better for you to lose one part of your body than for your whole body to be thrown into hell' (Matthew 5:29–30).
- **Murdering** 'Put to death, therefore, whatever belongs to your earthly nature: sexual immorality, impurity, lust, evil desires and greed, which is idolatry' (Colossians 3:5).

---

10 John Owen, 'Of the mortification of sin in believers', in *The Works of John Owen*, ed. William H. Goold (Edinburgh: T&T Clark, 1862), Vol. 6, p. 47, modernised.

- **Starving** 'Put on the Lord Jesus Christ, and make no provision for the flesh, to gratify its desires' (Romans 13:14, ESV).
- **Fighting** 'Take up the whole armour of God, that you may be able to withstand in the evil day, and having done all, to stand firm' (Ephesians 6:13–17, ESV).

As Paul exhorts Timothy to be godly, he uses three pictures that all highlight the effort involved.

- 'Train yourself to be godly' (1 Timothy 4:7–8). Imagine an athlete preparing for a race by following a strict diet. Each day they push themselves a little further. Often it hurts, but it's worth it to win the prize.
- 'Pursue righteousness, godliness, faith, love, endurance and gentleness' (1 Timothy 6:11). Imagine a lion in pursuit of an antelope. It's relentless as it follows the antelope, not giving up until it has it in its grasp.
- 'Fight the good fight of the faith' (1 Timothy 6:12). Now we're to imagine a boxer in the ring, taking heavy blows, but always getting up again to fight to the end.

We need to be violent with sin. If we hold back, it's almost certainly because we don't want to be violent towards something that we still love. We need to hate sin as sin and desire God for his own sake.

A cross-centred life

The key to change is continually returning to the cross. A changing life is a cross-centred life. At the cross we see the source of our sanctification (Ephesians 5:25; Colossians 1:22; Titus 2:14). We find hope, for we see the power of sin broken and the flesh with its sinful desires put to death. We see ourselves united to Christ and bought by his blood. We see the glorious grace of God, dying for his enemies, the righteous for the unrighteous. We see our hope, our life, our resources, our joy. If we don't come to the cross again and again, we'll feel distant from God, disconnected from his power and indifferent to his glory – and that is a recipe for sin.

A cross-centred life also means a resolute rejection of all self-confidence and self-righteousness. The life of Jesus shows us humility, but it is his cross that humbles us. At the cross we see the full extent of our sin: when we get the chance, we kill our Creator. The cross leaves no scope for human boasting. Instead, our only 'boast' is Christ Jesus, 'our righteousness, holiness and redemption' (1 Corinthians 1:30–31). Martyn Lloyd-Jones says:

> There is only one thing I know of that crushes me to the ground and humiliates me to the dust, and that is to look at the Son of God, and especially contemplate the cross . . . Nothing else can do it. When I see that I am a sinner . . . that nothing but the Son of God on the cross can save me, I'm humbled to the dust . . . Nothing but the cross can give us this spirit of humility.[11]

The secret of humility – and therefore of change – is never to stray far from the cross. It should often be in our thoughts, often on our lips, often in our songs, determining our actions, shaping our attitudes, captivating our affections.

When we go to the cross, we see our God dying for us. If you live for any other god then, when you fail, that god will beat you up for it. Suppose you live for people's approval or your career or possessions or control. What happens when you don't make it or you mess up? You're left afraid or downcast or bitter. But when you let Christ down, he still loves you. He doesn't beat you up; he's beaten up in your place. He doesn't make you suffer; he suffers in your place.

Look at the cross and see his love. Let that love win your love. Let that love replace any rival affections. The secret of change is to renew your love for Christ as you see him crucified in your place.

---

11 Cited in C. J. Mahaney, *Humility: True greatness* (Colorado Springs, CO: Multnomah, 2005), p. 66.

Reflection #1

John Owen exhorts us to bring our sinful desires to the gospel. 'Look on him whom you have pierced [Zechariah 12:10],' he says, 'and let your heart be disturbed by the sight.' Then he invites us to say to our souls:

What have I done? What love, what mercy, what blood, what grace have I despised and trampled on! Is this the response I make to the Father for his love, to the Son for his blood, to the Holy Spirit for his grace? Is this how I repay the Lord? Have I defiled the heart that Christ died to cleanse, and in which the blessed Spirit has chosen to dwell? Why can't I keep myself out of the dust? What can I say to the dear Lord Jesus? How shall I hold up my head with any boldness before him? Do I regard communion with him of so little value, that for the sake of this vile sin I have left him hardly any room in my heart? How shall I escape if I neglect so great a salvation in the future? And in the present, what shall I say to the Lord? Love, mercy, grace, goodness, peace, joy, consolation – I have despised them all, and valued them as nothing, that I might instead harbour sinful desires in my heart. Have I seen God as my Father simply so I might provoke him to his face? Was my soul washed clean to make room for new defilements? Shall I endeavour to frustrate the purposes of the death of Christ? Shall I daily grieve that Spirit through whom I am sealed to the day of redemption?[12]

Reflection #2

Puritan John Flavel identified six arguments that Satan uses to tempt us, together with six model responses.[13] Spot the voice of

---

12 John Owen, 'Of the mortification of sin in believers', *The Works of John Owen*, ed. William H. Goold (Edinburgh: T&T Clark, 1862), Vol. 6, p. 58.

13 Adapted from John Flavel, 'A saint indeed', in *The Works of John Flavel* (Edinburgh: Banner of Truth, 1968), Vol. 5, pp. 477–80. Also published as John Flavel, *Keeping the Heart* (Fearn, Ross-shire: Christian Heritage, 1999), pp. 116–21.

temptation in your life and identify how you should respond. You might like to ask two people to read it aloud as a dialogue.

Argument 1: The pleasure of sin

- **Temptation** Look at my smiling face and listen to my charming voice. Here is pleasure to be enjoyed. Who can stay away from such delights?
- **Response** The pleasures of sin are real, but so are the pangs of conscience and the flames of hell. The pleasures of sin are real, but pleasing God is much sweeter.

Argument 2: The secrecy of sin

- **Temptation** This sin will never disgrace you in public because no one will ever find out.
- **Response** Can you find somewhere God is not present for me to sin?

Argument 3: The profit of sin

- **Temptation** If you just stretch your conscience a little, you'll gain so much. This is your opportunity.
- **Response** What do I benefit if I gain the whole world but lose my own soul? I won't risk my soul for all I could have in this world.

Argument 4: The smallness of sin

- **Temptation** It's only a little thing, a small matter, a trifle. Who else would worry about such a trivial thing?
- **Response** Is the majesty of heaven a small matter too? If I commit this sin, I will offend and wrong our great God. Is there any little hell to torment little sinners? Great wrath awaits those the world thinks are little sinners. The littler the sin, the less reason there is to commit it! Why should I be unfaithful towards God for such a trifle?

Argument 5: The grace of God

- **Temptation** God will pass over this as a weakness. He won't make a big deal of it.

- **Response** Because God is good? Shall I take God's glorious mercy and make it a reason to sin? Shall I wrong him because he's good?

Argument 6: The example of others

- **Temptation** Better people than you have sinned in this way. And plenty of people have been restored after committing this sin.
- **Response** God didn't record the examples of good people sinning for me to copy, but to warn me. Am I willing to feel what they felt for sin? I dare not follow their example in case God plunges me into the depths of horror that he cast them.

Change project

7 What stops you changing?

Who or what do you blame for your sin?

Think about your change project. Do you ever hear yourself thinking or saying one of the following?

- They provoke me.
- If they'd only help me or love me more.
- I take after my parents.
- It's the way I am.
- People don't understand what it's like for me
- It's my background.
- It's so unfair.
- Anyone would have reacted the way I did.

Who or what do you blame for your behaviour or emotions?
Think about your change project. Is there someone else who feels guilty for your behaviour or emotions in this area? This may be because you've found ways of shifting the blame on to them.

How do you minimise your sin?

Think about your change project. Do you ever hear yourself thinking or saying one of the following?

- It's not that bad.
- It's only a small thing.
- What about what others do?
- Overall, I'm not too bad.
- Look at the good things I've done.
- Everyone else does it.
- It seemed the best thing to do.

How do you minimise your behaviour or emotions?

How do you avoid taking responsibility?

When you talk about your change project, do you ever say the following?

- 'I confess, but . . . ' What comes after the word 'but'?
- 'I would change if only . . . ' What comes after the words 'if only'?

Do you really want to change?

Do you just want to avoid the consequences of your sin or the shame of your sin?

Think about whether any of the following statements are true for you.[14]

- You want change, but without having to break a sweat.
- You want it because you're supposed to want it.
- You want it, but not at the cost of saying 'no' for ever.
- You want it – sometimes.
- You want it – tomorrow.

---

14 Adapted from Edward T. Welch, *Addictions: A banquet in the grave* (Phillipsburg, NJ: P&R Publishing, 2001), pp. 215–16.

- You want it, but you're waiting for God to remove your cravings first.
- You want it simply because it will make life easier.

In 2 Corinthians 7:10–11, Paul says:

> Godly sorrow brings repentance that leads to salvation and leaves no regret, but worldly sorrow brings death. See what this godly sorrow has produced in you: what earnestness, what eagerness to clear yourselves, what indignation, what alarm, what longing, what concern, what readiness to see justice done.

Does your repentance have the characteristics described in these verses?

- Are you earnest about holiness and eager to change?
- Are you indignant towards your sin and alarmed about where it might lead?
- Do you have a renewed longing for God and concern for holiness?
- Are you ready to put things right where you have wronged others?

Have you told someone?

- Have you asked someone to hold you accountable in your struggle? If not, then either you fear exposure more than you desire God or you still want to keep open the option to sin.
- Have you said, 'I'll tell someone if I ever do it again.' This is a stalling tactic. Get serious about change by telling someone now.

Write a summary of the ways you typically excuse, minimise or hide your sin so you can quickly spot them in future.

8

What strategies do you need to put in place to reinforce your faith and repentance?

By now you may have identified what lies behind your sinful behaviour or emotions and the truth you need to turn to in faith. You may have identified the idolatrous desires you need to turn from in repentance. Sadly, however, understanding doesn't equal change, though it can be a big step forward. This is because now we know what we need to do. Even if you've not fully analysed your heart – and there may be issues behind issues intersecting with other issues – you still know the gospel truths and gospel disciplines that will set you free. But the gospel disciplines of faith and repentance are a daily struggle. So Question 8 is, what strategies do you need to put in place to reinforce your faith and repentance?

> Do not be deceived: God cannot be mocked. A man reaps what he sows. Whoever sows to please their flesh, from the flesh will reap destruction; whoever sows to please the Spirit, from the Spirit will reap eternal life. (Galatians 6:7–8)

There is, says Paul, a principle in the world God has made: 'A man reaps what he sows' (v. 7b). It's true in agriculture and it's true in our spiritual lives. Only in fairy stories do you plant beans and reap magic stalks with treasure at the end. John Stott comments, 'This is a vitally important and much neglected principle of holiness. We are not helpless victims of our natures, temperament and environment. On the contrary, what we become depends largely on how we behave; our character is shaped by our conduct.'[1] Elsewhere Stott adds, 'We must not therefore be surprised if we do not reap the fruit of the Spirit when all the time we are sowing to the flesh. Did we think we could cheat or fool God?'[2]

What, then, does Paul mean by sowing to the flesh and sowing to the Spirit? He has just said,

> So I say, live by the Spirit, and you will not gratify the desires of the flesh. For the flesh desires what is contrary to the Spirit, and the Spirit what is contrary to the flesh. They are in conflict with each other, so that you are not to do whatever you want. (Galatians 5:16–17)

Our flesh has idolatrous desires that cause sinful behaviour and emotions. But the Spirit has placed a new desire in the heart of every Christian – the desire for holiness. So we sow to the flesh whenever we do something that strengthens or provokes our sinful desires. And we sow to the Spirit whenever we strengthen our Spirit-inspired desire for holiness.

We've seen that we can't change ourselves: it's God who changes us. But we participate in the process through faith and repentance. Faith and repentance are the only true gospel disciplines. It's important to see not sowing to the flesh and sowing to the Spirit in this context. They're not rules or disciplines re-entering by the back door. They address our heart and its desires. Not sowing to the flesh is all about reinforcing repentance. Sowing to the Spirit is about reinforcing faith.

- not sowing to the flesh = saying 'No' to whatever strengthens our sinful desires = reinforcing repentance
- sowing to the Spirit = saying 'Yes' to whatever strengthens our Spirit-inspired desires = reinforcing repentance.

---

1 John Stott, *The Message of Galatians* (Leicester: IVP, 1968), pp. 169–70.
2 John Stott with Tim Chester, *The Disciple: A calling to be Christlike* (London: IVP, 2019), p. 65.

Not sowing to the flesh

In order not to sow to our sinful natures, it can really help to avoid situations in which our sinful desires will be provoked. We can't change ourselves simply by avoiding temptation – rather, change must begin in our hearts. But avoiding temptation does have an important role to play. It's never the whole solution, but it's part of the solution. As my friend Samuel puts it, 'Avoidance buys us time.' Sometimes sinful desires *feel* strong, but if there's no stimulation for those desires, there's time for the truth to prevail in our hearts. We're particularly vulnerable to temptation when we're hungry, angry, lonely or tired (giving us the mnemonic 'HALT'). In these situations, we need to take special care. You may need to ensure that you have enough sleep or avoid being alone at key times.

The Bible talks about 'fleeing' temptation (1 Corinthians 6:18–20; 1 Timothy 6:9–11; 2 Timothy 2:22). We're to run in the opposite direction from anything that might strengthen or provoke our sinful desires. Teenagers commonly ask about dating, 'How far can I go?' It's a question many of us ask in other areas. 'What's acceptable?' 'Is it a sin if I only do this?' And God's answer is: 'RUN!' Don't ask, 'How far can I go towards sin?' Ask instead, 'How far can I run from sin?'

> No temptation has overtaken you except what is common to mankind. And God is faithful; he will not let you be tempted beyond what you can bear. But when you are tempted, he will also provide a way out so that you can endure it. Therefore, my dear friends, flee from idolatry.
> (1 Corinthians 10:13–14)

In every situation, God will provide a way to escape temptation, but that doesn't mean we can hang around in tempting situations or flirt with sinful desires. God provides an escape and '*therefore*' we should use it.

I have a friend who struggles with alcoholism. After a couple of pints, the alcohol seems to take over. By that point the battle is lost, but he can choose whether to go to the pub in the first place. God always gives us a way out before it's too late. We should take that escape route. And then run!

Saying 'No' to whatever strengthens our sinful desires

Most of our sinful desires can be fed by things in our culture. The lies behind our sins are lies perpetuated at a communal level. The Bible calls this influence 'the world'. Sometimes the Bible uses the term 'world' to describe the object of God's love (John 3:16), but it also uses this term to describe human society that is in opposition to God. The world around us celebrates sinful desires and spreads lies about God. We can't live in a ghetto, but we can and should take steps to reduce the world's influence on us.

> Do not love the world or anything in the world. If anyone loves the world, love for the Father is not in them. For everything in the world – the lust of the flesh, the lust of the eyes, and the pride of life – comes not from the Father but from the world. The world and its desires pass away, but whoever does the will of God lives for ever.
> (1 John 2:15–17)

I have a distinct memory that I've retained for more than twenty years. Some Christian friends and I had been talking about comedy we enjoyed, so I played them a favourite extract. I could immediately sense them wincing at the sexual innuendo. In that moment, I realised I'd been exposing myself to corrupting influences. God is not to be mocked. A man reaps what he sows. It proved a key moment in my Christian growth. We need to be willing to switch off the TV or disconnect from social media when their influences are unhelpful.

Traditionally, Christians have spoken of the world, the flesh and the devil as the three threats to a Christian life (Ephesians 2:1–3). They work together. The world is under the control of the evil one, so he spreads his lies through its culture (1 John 5:19). And these lies resonate with, and reinforce, the sinful desires of the flesh

(1 John 2:16). The question is, which voices are you listening to? The voices of the world, the flesh and the devil? Or the word of God?

The influence of social media

Social media is a fantastic way to enhance relationships. Home groups can organise meals through WhatsApp. Facebook enables us to publicise evangelistic events. Grandparents can enjoy pictures of their grandchildren. Missionaries can send prayer requests in real time.

But social media has a dark side. Studies have shown that it can increase depression and loneliness among many of its users. One reason is that the people we see on the various platforms seem to be having a much better time than us. Everyone is smiling. We forget that the edited highlights of our social media life look more fun than the mundane reality of our normal life. We look at other people's feeds and conclude that we're missing out. Meanwhile, they look at our feeds and think they're missing out. So social media can feed discontent.

It is also a shop window for unbiblical perspectives. Unbiblical views will start to feel normal if they're a regular feature of our feeds. Moreover, people say things on social media that they would never say to someone if they were in the same room together. On these platforms, the normal constraints of embodied life are removed, so conversations can become more heated and at times hateful. Or we get sucked into a bubble as the algorithms send us similar content to things we've liked and clicking on this new content prompts the algorithms to send more of the same in our direction. As a result, our ability to empathise with other perspectives can be eroded. Social media can distort our view.

Social media can also warp our priorities. Make-up videos may displace a concern for inner beauty. Or pages with collections of home interiors may make us unhappy with our home and lifestyle. Or we may fill our spare time with football chat. Or spend our money on what we are told is the latest must-have gear. There's nothing wrong with looking at any of these things, but if social media continually brings them to our attention, then our sense of what's *really* important can become distorted.

Psalm 1 describes how we can refocus and establish a right perspective:

> Blessed is the one
>   who does not walk in step with the wicked
> or stand in the way that sinners take
>   or sit in the company of mockers,
> but whose delight is in the law of the LORD,
>   and who meditates on his law day and night.
> That person is like a tree planted by streams of water,
>   which yields its fruit in season
> and whose leaf does not wither –
>   whatever they do prospers.
> (Psalm 1:1–3)

Do you want to be spiritually refreshed (planted by streams), fruitful (yielding fruit in season) and stable (not withering)? Then you need to spend time in God's word, delighting in his law and hearing his voice (v. 2). But you also need to avoid the harmful influences of the world around you (v. 1). Of course we shouldn't avoid encountering people of other faiths or none. Quite the opposite: we're called to serve and witness in the world around us. But the psalmist is talking here about sitting under their influence. If harmful voices are a regular part of our lives, then their wickedness and mockery will come to seem normal to us.

The way social media works can also make it harder for us to grow as Christians. The genius of social media is that it allows me to be at the centre of my world – a world that I curate. This is what makes it so attractive. It reinforces our in-built bias towards the self. In contrast, the real world constantly reminds me that I'm *not* at its centre. Put me in a crowded room and it's obvious that, for this group of people, the world does not revolve around me. Real-world interactions also mean people can see me as I really am. This is the joy of Christian community: people both accept me as I really am and help me to become who I should be. The Church is 'a chosen people' – a people chosen by God, not by me (1 Peter 2:9). In the real world, God places other people in my life to serve me and to be served by me.

'Likes' in the digital world have become a way of gaining approval and measuring our standing (our righteousness in the eyes of the world). You create or curate a version of yourself to win the approval of others. It's a form of salvation by works. The good news is that we don't need to self-create our identity. It is given to us by God through faith in Christ. God looks at our life – not just the curated version, but the real version with all its dark secrets – and he clicks 'like'.[3]

So avoiding whatever provokes or strengthens sinful desires might include a review of the way you use social media.

Some other practical steps we can take

What does it mean in practice to say 'No' to whatever might provoke or strengthen our sinful desires? Here are some examples of what is possible.

Jack struggled with lust. He realised that he had to stop undressing women with his eyes, choosing films with sex scenes and watching late-night television on his own. When he did see sexual images, he made an effort to think about the goodness of God. He installed anti-porn software on his computer and got a friend to ask him 'the question' on a regular basis.

Carla struggled with the desire to be loved. So she decided to stop flirting, for the kick it gave her. Out went her low-cut tops and short skirts. She stopped watching romantic films, reading romantic fiction and daydreaming about marriage.

Colin's desire for control was making him an anxious and demanding manager. To counter this, he stopped monitoring tasks that he'd delegated to colleagues. At first, he worried about them,

---

3 For a Christian perspective on social media, see Tim Chester, *Will You Be My Facebook Friend?: Social media and the gospel* (Leyland: 10Publishing, 2018).

but he refused to let himself check up on people. He bought a second phone for personal use and switched his work phone off at weekends. He decided not to plan his Saturdays, but take them as they came.

Emma found refuge in shopping. So she unsubscribed from fashion-related social media feeds and stopped buying glossy magazines. She only went shopping when she needed something and always made a list.

Jamal knew that he had a tendency to be self-absorbed. So he stopped updating his social media feeds because they encouraged him to focus on himself. He also stopped having fantasies in which he was the hero. Instead, he started volunteering at a local shelter helping homeless people.

Alcohol was an issue for Kate. So she decided to stop drinking any alcohol at all. She avoided pubs and friends who encouraged her to drink. If she did spend time with those friends, she'd take a Christian friend with her.

Not all these actions will be appropriate for you – we each struggle with different sinful desires. Something one person needs to avoid might be 'safe' for someone else. I desire to control the future, which makes me cautious about money, so I decided to stop keeping a record of spending to help me be freer with money. Someone else might satisfy a desire for meaning and satisfaction by shopping, so keeping a record of spending might be a great thing for them to do. These suggestions, therefore, are *not* marks of a Christlike life. You've got to work out what strategies *you* need to adopt to avoid provoking your own sinful desires and minimise the impact of the wider culture on how you live. John Stott sums it up well:

To 'sow to the flesh' is to pander to it, to cosset, cuddle and stroke it, instead of crucifying it . . . Every time we allow our mind to harbour a grudge, nurse a grievance, entertain an impure fantasy or wallow in self-pity, we are sowing to the flesh. Every time we linger in bad company whose insidious influence we know we cannot resist, every time we lie in bed when we ought to be up and praying, every time we read pornographic literature, every time we take a risk which strains our self-control, we are sowing, sowing, sowing to the flesh. Some Christians sow to the flesh every day and wonder why they do not reap holiness.[4]

This can be a hard ask. Jesus compares it to amputation (Matthew 5:29–30)! We're likely to feel loss, even grief, when we think about what we must do to starve our sinful desires. These desires can seem like old friends, ones we've loved for many years, and nobody likes killing off their best friends! One man said to me as we discussed what he needed to do, 'I feel like I'll be losing a bit of my heart.' I was about to qualify his statement to him when I realised that it's exactly like losing a bit of your heart! There's a bit of my heart that is attached to my sinful desires and I need some surgery to remove it.

In a famous sermon entitled 'The expulsive power of a new affection', Thomas Chalmers argued that we can't simply tell ourselves to stop sinning. We need to direct the desires that sin falsely claims to satisfy towards that which truly satisfies and liberates: God himself. A renewed affection for God is the only thing that will expel sinful desires. We're like a child holding a rusty knife. What we grasp endangers us, but we don't want to let it go. If you shout at the child long enough, they might reluctantly hand it over. But offer them a lovely new toy and the knife is soon forgotten. *Tell* someone to stop sinning and, at best, they may do so reluctantly and partially. But give them a vision of knowing God and his glory, and they'll gladly root out all that gets in the way of their relationship with God (Hebrews 12:1–3).

Sowing to the Spirit

Sowing to the Spirit is about cultivating this new affection for God with its power to expel sinful desires. The best way to avoid weeds in your garden is to sow other plants in their place. It's the same in

---

4   John Stott, *The Message of Galatians* (Leicester: IVP, 1968), p. 170.

our spiritual life. The best way to keep down our sinful desires is to sow to the Spirit. When Paul tells Timothy to flee sinful desire, he also tells him to pursue righteousness in its place. 'For the love of money is a root of all kinds of evil . . . But you, man of God, flee from all this, and pursue righteousness, godliness, faith, love, endurance and gentleness' (1 Timothy 6:10). 'Flee the evil desires of youth, and pursue righteousness, faith, love and peace, along with those who call on the Lord out of a pure heart' (2 Timothy 2:22).

Saying 'Yes' to whatever strengthens our Spirit-inspired desires

Sowing to the Spirit means doing exactly this. As we've seen, we sin when we believe lies about God. Sowing to the Spirit means *filling our hearts with the truth about God*. We sin because sinful desires matter more to us than God. We sow to the Spirit when we cultivate our love for God.

I shall describe eight things that do this and so reinforce our faith. Sometimes people call these 'spiritual disciplines', but I believe that this terminology is unhelpful. It can make Christian growth seem like an achievement on our part. In reality it's God who changes us through his grace. The only true spiritual disciplines in the Christian life are faith and repentance – actions that direct our attention to God's gracious activity. So, instead, I prefer the traditional term: 'the means of grace'. Or a better term might be 'the means of communion'.[5] These are ways in which we enjoy and strengthen our relationship with God, and if we're walking closely with God, then we're less likely to walk the path of sin. These are gifts that God graciously gives and uses to strengthen his work of grace in our hearts. They are the means by which God feeds our faith in him.[6] This is what sowing to the Spirit looks like in practice.

---

5 Tim Chester, *Enjoying God: Experience the power and love of God in everyday life* (Epsom: The Good Book Company, 2018), pp. 132–4.

6 J. C. Ryle, *Holiness: Its nature, hindrances, difficulties and roots* (Cambridge: James Clarke, 1956), p. 21.

1 The Bible

The word of God is perhaps God's primary means of changing us: 'Sanctify them by the truth,' prays Jesus, adding 'your word is truth' (John 17:17). The Bible is the:

- water by which we're washed (Ephesians 5:26)
- weapon and armour for our fight (Ephesians 6:14–17)
- toolkit with which we're equipped (2 Timothy 3:16)
- milk that enables us to grow (1 Peter 2:2).

The link between our hearts and behaviour is fine in theory, but perhaps when you look at your own heart, you see only muddle and confusion. You can't work out the desires that rule your heart, nor spot the lies that shape your behaviour. But

> the word of God is alive and active. Sharper than any double-edged sword, it penetrates even to dividing soul and spirit, joints and marrow; it judges the thoughts and attitudes of the heart. Nothing in all creation is hidden from God's sight. Everything is uncovered and laid bare before the eyes of him to whom we must give account.
> (Hebrews 4:12–13)

> The Bible is like God's great scalpel. It is able to cut through all the layers of who I am and what I'm doing to expose my heart . . . The Bible by its very nature is heart-revealing. For that reason, Scripture must be our central tool in personal growth and ministry.[7]

James describes the Bible as a mirror in which we see ourselves as we really are (James 1:22–25). We should read the Bible not simply that we might expound it, but that it might expound us.

More important than revealing our hearts, the Bible reveals

---

7 Paul Tripp and Timothy Lane, *Helping Others Change* (Greensboro, NC: New Growth Press, 2005), 2.7.

Christ's glory. We're changed as we see the glory of God revealed in Christ (2 Corinthians 3:18), and we see the light of the glory of Christ in the gospel word (4:4–6).

So the Bible speaks liberating truth to our enslaved hearts, both as we read it for ourselves and as we hear it preached. If we are not 'in' the Bible day by day, then our hearts will be immersed only in the lies of our culture. The Bible is the source of truth that counters the lies of sin: 'He that would be holy must steep himself in the Word, must bask in the sunshine which radiates from each page of revelation.'[8]

> The law of the LORD is perfect,
>   refreshing the soul.
> The statutes of the LORD are trustworthy,
>   making wise the simple.
> The precepts of the LORD are right,
>   giving joy to the heart.
> The commands of the LORD are radiant,
>   giving light to the eyes.
> (Psalm 19:7–8)

You may feel that your soul is sick, confused or downcast. You may be troubled by worry, sin, problems, suffering, fear or guilt. In the word of God, you will find medicine for your soul. But don't wait until this happens – prevention is better than cure. The Bible offers a healthy diet of truth that can prevent problems arising in the first place: 'I have hidden your word in my heart,' says Psalm 119:11, 'that I might not sin against you.' Chris Wright comments, 'The more we instil the Bible into our heart, mind, soul and bloodstream, the harder we will find it to sin comfortably. The Bible enlivens our conscience and drives us back to God in repentance and a longing to live as it pleases him.'[9] The Bible, by revealing the glory of Christ, reinforces our new Spirit-given desires.

---

8 Horatius Bonar, *God's Way of Holiness* (Darlington: Evangelical Press, 1979), pp. 5–6.
9 Christopher J. H. Wright, *Life Through God's Word: Psalm 119* (Carlisle: Authentic, 2006), p. 65.

Again and again, I've traced a correlation in my life between a neglect of God's word and spiritual weakness. It's not that the Bible is a magic cure for sin or a talisman against temptation. Instead, the Bible contains the truth about God's greatness and goodness that undermines the lies of sin. So, don't merely read it each day as a duty to tick off. Savour the truth of God that it reveals. Look for the glory of Christ. Let it interpret your heart. Meditate on what you read. Pray it through. Read it not simply to be informed but also to be transformed and conformed to the likeness of Jesus (Romans 12:2).

2 Prayer

As important as it is, the word of God on its own will not bring about change. Plenty of people hear God's word being preached and remain completely unmoved by it. Even as Christians, we've all had plenty of times when we've read the Bible or heard it preached and not really engaged with it. We need eyes to see and ears to hear. We need God himself to be at work as we read. And that's what God has promised to do through the Holy Spirit. But, of course, we can't 'do' the Spirit. The Spirit is not a button we can press to make change happen. What we can do, though, is *pray*. At the heart of all Christian ministry – and personal change is no exception – are the word and prayer. We need to pray that the Spirit of God will use the word of God to recapture our hearts for Christ.

We often complain that we lack time to pray, but everyone has twenty-four hours each day. People who pray more don't secretly have twenty-five hours. Our problem is that we decide other things are more important. But when we realise God is the great change agent in our lives, prayer will inevitably move up the priority list. For some this will require 'planned neglect' – deciding to neglect other activities. J. C. Ryle says:

> Praying and sinning will never live together in the same heart. Prayer will consume sin, or sin will choke prayer . . . *Diligence in prayer is the secret of eminent holiness*. Without controversy there is a vast difference among true Christians . . . I believe the difference in nineteen cases out of twenty arises from

different habits about private prayer. I believe that those who are not eminently holy pray *little*, and those who are eminently holy pray *much*.[10]

We should also make prayer our natural recourse in times of temptation. When we see a sexy image, when anger rises in our hearts, when we feel despondent – in all these situations and many more, we should shoot a prayer up to God. A child will play happily in their own little world, but as soon as they sense danger, they'll look around for their parent. This is how it should be for us as children of God. As soon as we sense danger, we should look up to our heavenly Father for help.

3 Community

One of the reasons God has put us in Christian communities is to help us to change. The Church is to be a community of change. We'll think more about this in Chapter 9, but here are some ways in which the Church is a means of grace.

- We remind one another of the truth.
- We are taught the Bible by people God has gifted for that purpose.
- We pray together for God's help.
- We model Christian change and holiness for one another.
- We see God at work in the lives of others.
- We can point out one another's blind spots.
- We remind one another of God's greatness and goodness as we worship him together.
- We are given opportunities for service.
- We provide accountability for one another.

4 Worship

In congregational worship, we're reminding ourselves that God is bigger and better than anything sin offers. Worship isn't just an affirmation that God is good, it's an affirmation that God is *better*. In

---

10 J. C. Ryle, *Practical Religion* (Edinburgh: Banner of Truth, 1998), pp. 71 and 74–5.

worship, we don't just call on one another to worship God, we also call one another *away* from worshipping other gods. We remind our hearts of God's greatness, glory, goodness and grace ('the four Gs' of Chapter 5). This isn't only an intellectual recalling – God has also given us music to touch our emotions. We sing the truth so that it moves us, inspires us, stirs us, encourages us and transforms us.

Have you ever got the tune of a mindless song stuck in your head? You find yourself humming a song that you don't even like. The world around us sings a song and it often gets stuck in our head. We find ourselves joining in. What the world thinks and desires becomes what we think and desire. To worship God is to retune our hearts.

5 The Lord's Supper

One special means of grace is Communion, or, the Lord's Supper.[11] The bread and wine remind us that Christ gave his life to make us holy, to break the power of sin, to give us a new identity, to make us family. They remind us that we belong to God because we were bought and the price was Christ's blood. More than this, Christ himself is present with us through his Spirit. The bread and wine are physical tokens of Christ's spiritual presence. Christ didn't simply give us words to say or ideas to remember. Knowing how frail and fragile we are, he graciously gave us bread and wine to strengthen our faith and captivate our hearts. Sinclair Ferguson says, 'We do not get a different or a better Christ in the sacraments than we do in the Word . . . But we may get the same Christ better, with a firmer grasp of his grace through seeing, touching, feeling, and tasting as well as hearing.'[12] So the Book of Common Prayer summons us to 'feed on him in your heart by faith with thanksgiving.'[13] The Lord's Supper is a fresh invitation to 'Taste

---

11 See Tim Chester, *Truth We Can Touch: How baptism and Communion shape our lives* (Wheaton, IL: Crossway, 2020).

12 Sinclair B. Ferguson, *The Whole Christ* (Wheaton, IL: Crossway, 2016), p. 223. See also John Calvin, *Institutes of the Christian Religion*, ed. John T. McNeill, trans. Ford Lewis Battles (Philadelphia, PA/London: Westminster/SCM Press, 1961), 4.14.3, 5–6.

13 'The order for the administration of the Holy Communion', in The Book of Common Prayer (1662) (Cambridge: Cambridge University Press, 2004), p. 256.

and see that the LORD is good' (Psalm 34:8). We discover again the promise of Jesus: 'I am the bread of life. Whoever comes to me will never go hungry, and whoever believes in me will never be thirsty' (John 6:35). We renew communion with Jesus by faith. We're reminded of the truth that the bread and wine represent and this truth feeds our hearts.

6 Service

We often think of serving others as the fruit of change, but it's also a means of grace and God can use it to change us. Here's how this works. Fundamentally, sin is an orientation towards the self. Many of us suffer from self-absorption. We're preoccupied with our problems and successes. We bring every conversation round to our favourite subject: ourselves. Or we develop habits of self-centredness, in which we live for our own comfort and security. Serving God and other people can help to redirect us outwards, taking our attention away from ourselves. It's a great prescription for people experiencing negative emotions. This is why Paul's advice to a thief is not just 'stop stealing' but do 'something useful with their own hands, that they may have something to share with those in need' (Ephesians 4:28). Paul wants people to stop thinking about their wants and to start thinking about other people's needs.

All sorts of things can happen when we start serving others. We learn from them. We see God at work in their lives. We find joy in serving God. We see prayer being answered. We face situations we can't cope with and discover God's strength. We discover the excitement of seeing God glorified in people's lives.

if you pour yourself out for the hungry
    and satisfy the desire of the afflicted,
then shall your light rise in the darkness
    and your gloom be as the noonday.
And the LORD will guide you continually
    and satisfy your desire in scorched places
and make your bones strong;

and you shall be like a watered garden,
　　like a spring of water,
　　whose waters do not fail.
(Isaiah 58:10–11, ESV)

What is God's promise to the gloomy, the uncertain, the dissatis-
fied, the weary, the dry? He will lift the gloom, guide us, satisfy our
desires, strengthen our bones, water our hearts if we give ourselves
in service to the poor. God made us to love him and love others,
so we become the people we were meant to be by serving others.
When you 'pour yourself out' (v. 10), you will find yourself filled
up. If you 'satisfy the desire of the afflicted,' then God will 'satisfy
your desires in scorched places' (vv. 10, 11).

7 Suffering

In the film *The Karate Kid*, a young student is set a series of tasks by
the old master – painting the fence, cleaning the car and so on. The
boy thinks that they're all meaningless and irrelevant. But, eventu-
ally, he discovers that the repeated hand and arm movements have
given him strength, reflexes and agility – everything he needs to be
a great karate fighter!

Often, the events of our lives appear meaningless and irrelevant
but, all the time, God is training us in grace and godliness. Even
suffering is a means of grace in the hands of God. In Judges 3:1–2,
God leaves other nations in the promised land 'to teach warfare'
to his people. As each generation confronted hostile armies, it
was faced with the need to trust God for itself. Adversity tests,
strengthens and personalises faith.

Sinful desires can lurk in our hearts unnoticed because those
desires are neither threatened nor thwarted. But suffering stirs
the calm waters of latent sinful desires. It reveals the true state of
our hearts. It's God's diagnostic tool, preparing the way for the
medicine of gospel truth. Deuteronomy 8:2 (ESV) says, 'you shall
remember the whole way that the LORD your God has led you these
forty years in the wilderness, that he might humble you, testing you
to know what was in your heart'. Horatius Bonar comments:

The trial did not create the evil: it merely brought out what was there already, unnoticed and unfelt, like a torpid adder. Then the heart's deep fountains were broken up, and streams of pollution came rushing out, black as Hell . . . Even so it is with the saints still. God chastens them that He may draw forth the evil that is lying concealed and unsuspected within . . . When calamity breaks over them like a tempest, then the hidden evils of their heart awaken.[14]

So suffering always presents us with a choice. We can get frustrated, angry, bitter or despondent as our desire for control, success, love or health is threatened. Or we can hold on to God in a new way, finding our joy in him and comfort in his promises.

On 19 May 2006, Nicole Tripp was hit by a car, which crushed her against a wall, seriously injuring her. In that moment, her life and the life of her parents was turned upside down. Their days were then dominated by the slow routine of her recovery. Her father, author and counsellor Paul Tripp, wrote a blog to keep friends informed of her progress. Here's one entry:

It's hard not to look at the day as a day of futile activity accompanied by needless discomfort. You can't honestly look at the day and make sense out of it . . . Suffering transports you beyond the boundaries of your reason and your control . . . Suffering is a kidnapper that comes into our lives, blindfolds us, and takes us to where we do not want to be.

But suffering is not just a kidnapper, it is also a teacher . . . It points you to the fact that there is little that you actually control. It instructs you as to where reliable comfort and sturdy hope can be found. Like a patient teacher with a resistant student, suffering pries open your hands and asks you to let go of your life. Suffering invites you to find security, rest, hope, and comfort in Another, and in so doing, assaults the irrationality

---

14 Horatius Bonar, 'The night of weeping', in *The Life and Works of Horatius Bonar* (Toronto: LUX Publications, 2004), pp. 36–7.

of personal sovereignty that is the delusion of every human being. In that way, suffering is not just a kidnapper, and not just a teacher, it is also a liberator. Suffering frees us to experience a deeper comfort and hope than we have ever had before.[15]

8 Hope

John Calvin commends what he calls the 'meditation on the future life'.[16] We need to dream of the new creation. We need to remind one another of the 'eternal glory' that awaits us and far outweighs 'our light and momentary troubles' (2 Corinthians 4:17–18; Romans 8:17–18). This means recalling that we're pilgrims in this world, passing through on the way to 'a better country' (Hebrews 11:13–16; 1 Peter 1:1, 2:11). 'Although believers are now pilgrims on earth,' says Calvin, 'yet by their confidence they surmount the heavens, so that they cherish their future inheritance in their bosoms with tranquillity.'[17] What frees us from the vain pursuit of earthly treasure is the hope of treasure in heaven (Matthew 6:19–20; 1 Timothy 6:17–19).

Our meditation on the future life is closely linked with the ascension of Christ. By faith, we're united with the ascended and glorified Christ. So we fix our eyes on his heavenly glory. 'Since, then, you have been raised with Christ, set your hearts on things above, where Christ is, seated at the right hand of God' (Colossians 3:1). It's with eyes fixed on heavenly things that we 'Put to death . . . whatever belongs to [our] earthly nature' (v. 5). Thinking of Christ's return loosens the hold that the world has on us and inspires us to change (2 Peter 3:10–14; 1 John 3:2–3).

---

15 Paul David Tripp, 'Control?', nicolenews.blogspot.com, 11 June 2006.

16 John Calvin, *Institutes of the Christian Religion*, ed. John T. McNeill, trans. Ford Lewis Battles (Philadelphia, PA/London: Westminster/SCM Press, 1961), 3.9.1.

17 John Calvin, *Commentary on the Epistles of Paul the Apostle to the Romans and to the Thessalonians*, ed. David W. Torrance and Thomas F. Torrance, trans. Ross Mackenzie (Edinburgh: St Andrew Press, 1961), comments on Romans 5:2, p. 105.

Reflection #1

Look up the following list of Paul's prayers.

- Romans 15:5–6, 13
- 2 Corinthians 13:14
- Ephesians 1:17–19; 3:16–21
- Philippians 1:9–11
- Colossians 1:9–14
- 1 Thessalonians 3:9–13
- 2 Thessalonians 1:11–12; 2:16–17
- Philemon 1:4–6.

For what does Paul pray? How do these compare with the sorts of things for which you typically pray?

Reflection #2

Do you make the most of the 'means of grace'? Are any of the following things that you could do? Identify three things you want to start doing or do differently to strengthen your faith.

- Make the Bible part of your daily routine.
- Turn to the Bible when you feel tempted or under pressure.
- Listen to the Bible being read, using an app or audiobook.
- Study the Bible regularly with another Christian.
- Write out Bible verses to meditate on during the day.
- Memorise Bible verses – especially ones that counter the lies behind your sins.
- Carry a copy of the New Testament with you, so that you can read it in idle moments.
- Read a book that helps you to understand the Bible or inspires you to live as a Christian.
- Make prayer part of your daily routine.
- Pray when you feel tempted or under pressure.
- Pray regularly with another Christian.

- Attend the meetings of your church.
- Make the most of Bible teaching in church.
- Meet up with other Christians throughout the week.
- Attend the Lord's Supper to commune with Christ.
- Talk with other Christians about your struggle with sin.
- Encourage other Christians with the truth.
- Make praise part of your daily routine (even if you can't sing well).
- Listen to Christian music that strengthens your faith.
- Thank God throughout the day for his blessings.
- Find ways to serve people.
- Volunteer for a church or community project.
- Regard your suffering as a gift from God.
- Comfort others with the comfort you have received in your suffering.
- Think and talk often of heaven.

Change project

Question 8: What strategies do you need to put in place to reinforce your faith and repentance?

What can you do to avoid provoking sinful desires?

Think about the issue you have chosen for your change project.

- In what location are you most likely to do it or feel it?
- At what time?
- With which people?
- Do hunger, anger, loneliness or tiredness make you more vulnerable to temptation?

What steps can you take to reduce temptation in your life?

What can you do to avoid strengthening sinful desires?

Think about the area you have chosen for your change project.

- Which images, films, TV programmes, books, magazines and social media feeds strengthen your sinful desires?
- Which people strengthen your sinful desires?
- Which activities strengthen your sinful desires?
- Think about the lies behind your behaviour or emotions (see your answer to Question 5 in Chapter 5). When do you see or hear those lies?

Is your use of social media helping or hindering your spiritual growth?

- Does your social media self accurately reflect your real self?
- Is your use of social media enhancing real-world relationships or replacing them?
- Is your use of social media reinforcing biblical truths or making biblical truths seem outdated?
- How does your use of social media affect your change project?

What steps can you take to ensure your sinful desires are not strengthened?

If you're not sure about an activity or situation, then use these questions, based on 1 Corinthians 6:12 and 10:23–24.

- Is this activity beneficial? Does it help me become more like Jesus?
- Is this activity mastering me? Does it strengthen a desire that might control my heart?
- Is this activity constructive? Is it good for others? Might it cause another Christian to be tempted?

What can you do to strengthen your faith?

Do you make the most of the 'means of grace'? Identify five practical steps you will start taking or things you will do differently to strengthen your faith through the means of grace.

Write a summary of the strategies you plan to adopt to reinforce your faith and repentance.

9

How can we support one another in change?

He'd passed up the opportunity a hundred times before but, taking himself by surprise, he decided to go for it today. He spluttered that he had something to say. Now he was beyond the point of no return. There were four other people round the table at their lunchtime prayer meeting, all looking at him warmly. He took a deep breath and told them – confessing his sin, confessing years of sin. For Stephen, it was a turning point. Three years later, that moment is still etched on his mind. But those three years have been ones of joy and freedom and growth.

God is in the business of change and he's placed us in a community of change. The Church is one of God's means of grace, reinforcing our faith and repentance, but it's also a channel for the other means of grace. Change in the Bible is not a solo project; it's a community project. Gary Millar says, 'We are changed in the context of the *church*. God has designed the local church to be the network of relationships in which we are forced to learn to love, forgive, repent, mourn, build up, rebuke and encourage.'[1]

In this chapter, we'll look at how you can be helped to change by your church. But we'll also consider the role you can play in helping others to change.

A community of change

The Christian community is the best context for change because it's the context *God himself* has given. That means it's a better place

---

1 J. Gary Millar, *Changed into His Likeness: A biblical theology of personal transformation* (London: IVP, 2021), p. 238.

for change than a therapy group, a counsellor's office or a retreat centre. We grasp the love of Christ 'together with all the Lord's holy people' (Ephesians 3:18). Christ gives gifts to the Church so that we can grow together (4:7–13).

What does Christian maturity look like? It looks like Jesus (vv. 13, 15). And one of the great things about the Christian community is that it gives us models of Christlike behaviour. Of course, no one is perfectly like Jesus (except Jesus), but other Christians help us to see what it means to walk with God. It's not just godliness we model for one another but also growth and grace. We model growth when people see us struggling with sin and turning in faith to God. Every Sunday in our little church we give people the opportunity to talk about what God has been doing in their lives during the past week – answers to prayer, comfort from God's word, opportunities for evangelism, help with temptation. In so doing, we reinforce our belief in a God who is alive and active among us.

One reason the ascended Christ gave the Spirit to the Church is to equip each of us with a special gift – our contribution to the life of this community (v. 7). So everyone's contribution matters: 'From [Christ] the whole body, joined and held together by every supporting ligament, grows and builds itself up in love, *as each part does its work*' (v. 16). We all have a role to play. We need one another for the Church to be healthy and grow. That means everyone else needs you and you need everyone else. You need to help others change and you need to let them help you.

Together we extol Christ to one another and we each bring distinct harmonies to the song. We comfort one another with the comfort we have received (2 Corinthians 1:3–7). Our different experiences of God's grace become part of the rich counsel that we have for one another. Moreover, in the Christian community, there is a collective persistence that's stronger than any individual can manage alone. When I grow weary of speaking truth to a particular situation, someone else can take up the baton. We're like a choir singing the praises of Jesus. No one can sustain the song continually on their own, but together we can.

Paul particularly highlights the role of those who proclaim, explain and apply God's word (Ephesians 4:11). That's because the Bible is the source of the truth about God that counters the lies behind our sin. But notice, it's not these leaders who do the work of God in the Church. Their role is to equip God's people, for it's they who do the 'works of service' (vv. 11–12). It's God's people who together build up the body of Christ.[2] We work with one another and for one another so that, together, we can be mature and Christlike.

Paul says that Christ 'makes the whole body fit together perfectly' (v. 16, NLT). Your church is not a collection of random people. Christ has specially selected each one to create a perfect fit. You may have chosen other people, but God placed these people in your life to help you change. As my friend Matt said when we were talking about Ephesians 4, 'I need to give everyone in our church a new merit in my life.'

Paul isn't talking in Ephesians 4 about an idealised church with idealised people. He's writing to a real church with real people. He's talking about *your* church. You can't say, 'Fine in theory, but my church is never going to be like that.' God has given these people to you so they can care for you and you can care for them. If your church isn't what it should be, then start changing it – start sharing your struggles and start speaking the truth in love to others.

Verse 31 says, 'Get rid of all bitterness, rage and anger, brawling and slander, along with every form of malice.' These behaviours all have two things in common. First, they involve other people. Second, they're symptoms of threatened or thwarted sinful desires. Often, we can't spot our sinful desires. But when they're threatened or thwarted by other people, we respond with bitterness, rage, anger, brawling, slander and malice. One of the great things about living as part of a community is that, in community, people bump into your idols. People press your buttons. They wind you up. That's when we respond with bitterness, rage and so on. And that enables

---

2 For a more a detailed discussion of these verses, see Peter T. O'Brien, *The Letter to the Ephesians* (Grand Rapids, MI/Nottingham: Eerdmans/Apollos, 1999), pp. 297–305.

us to spot our idolatrous desires. God is using the different people, including the people you don't naturally get on with (perhaps them most of all), to change your heart. He's placed you together so you can rub off each other's rough edges. It's as though God has placed us like rocks in a bag and is shaking us about so we collide with one another. Sometimes sparks fly but, gradually, we become beautiful, smooth gemstones. Remember next time someone is rubbing you up the wrong way that God is smoothing you! God has given you that person in love, as a gift to make you holy. Sinclair Ferguson comments:

> The church is a community in which we receive spiritual help, but also one in which deep-seated problems will come to the surface and will require treatment . . . we often discover things about our own hearts which we never anticipated.[3]

A community of truth

How do we grow more like Christ? We've seen that we become mature 'in the faith and in the knowledge of the Son of God,' as Paul puts it in verse 13. Immaturity involves being 'tossed and blown about by every wind of new teaching', susceptible to 'lies so clever they sound like the truth' (v. 14, NLT). The world, the flesh and the devil whisper lies that sound plausible. Maturity is being able to say, 'No, that's not the truth about God. I'm not going to think or behave that way.'

This means that we grow towards maturity by 'speaking the truth in love' to one another (v. 15). We build one another up through the words we say. So we need to be intentional with our words: 'Do not let any unwholesome talk come out of your mouths, but only what is helpful for building others up according to their needs, that it may benefit those who listen' (v. 29). We need to be communities in which we encourage, challenge, console, counsel, exhort and comfort one another with the truth. We need to be communities in which everyone is speaking truth to everyone.

---

3 Sinclair B. Ferguson, *Grow in Grace* (Edinburgh: Banner of Truth, 1989), p. 77.

Paul reminds us why 'speaking the truth in love' is so central to change. He reminds us first that the underlying causes of sinful behaviour and negative emotions are futile thinking, darkened understanding, ignorant minds, hardened hearts and indulged desires (vv. 17–19). In other words, we think or believe lies instead of trusting God's word (as we saw in Chapter 5) and we desire or worship idols instead of worshipping God (see Chapter 6). Paul continues:

> That, however, is not the way of life you learned when you heard about Christ and were taught in him in accordance with the truth that is in Jesus. You were taught, with regard to your former way of life, to put off your old self, which is being corrupted by its deceitful desires; to be made new in the attitude of your minds; and to put on the new self, created to be like God in true righteousness and holiness.
> (Ephesians 4:20–24)

What changes us is the truth. That's what Paul spotlights: 'heard', 'taught', 'truth'– all that you might 'be made new in the attitude of your minds' (v. 20). The problem is 'deceitful desires' (v. 22) – desires that purport to offer more than God but, in fact, only enslave us. The answer is 'the truth that is in Jesus' (v. 21). The truth of Jesus sets us free by giving us new desires for God.

So Paul says to the people of the church at Ephesus: 'Therefore each of you must put off falsehood and speak truthfully to your neighbour, for we are all members of one body' (v. 25). Paul isn't simply saying, 'Don't tell fibs.' You're to 'put off' falsehood just as you 'put off your old self' (v. 22). We're to stop perpetrating lies that lead to sinful desires. Instead of affirming people's deceitful desires, we're to remind one another of the greatness and goodness of God revealed in Jesus.

'Let us consider how we may spur one another on towards love and good deeds,' says Hebrews 10:24–25, 'not giving up meeting together, as some are in the habit of doing, but encouraging one another – and all the more as you see the Day approaching.' We meet together so we can encourage *one another*. We're to address psalms, hymns and spiritual songs '*to one another*' (Ephesians 5:19–20).

Our Sunday gatherings have a particular role to play in this. This is where we hear God's word being preached. This is where that truth is reinforced in the songs we sing. This is where that truth is on display in bread and wine. But it goes beyond attending church each Sunday. Every day, the world, the flesh and the devil perpetrate deceitful desires. So I need a daily dose of truth. That's why Hebrews 3:12–13 says, 'See to it, brothers and sisters, that none of you has a sinful, unbelieving heart that turns away from the living God. But encourage one another daily, as long as it is called "Today", so that none of you may be hardened by sin's deceitfulness.' We're to encourage one another *daily*. Every day our hearts teeter on the brink of becoming sinful, unbelieving, hardened and deceived. Through the week, we need people who will speak truth to us.

Sometimes you hear people say, 'You mustn't let other Christians become a crutch you lean on.' I don't buy it. We're (rightly) urged to read our Bibles every day without anyone complaining that this makes the Bible a crutch. If we were ever to face solitary confinement, then I'm sure God would prove himself sufficient for us. But in the meantime, God himself has given us both the Bible and the Christian community to help us persevere and grow. What we do need to watch is becoming dependent on a particular individual. That's nearly always unhealthy. Christ is our Saviour and we need people to point us to him. But what we don't want is substitute saviours – people who solve our problems or give us reassurance when we should be looking to Christ. God has given us the Christian community not as a substitute for Christ but as a pointer to Christ. The truth we speak to one another is 'the truth that is in Jesus' (Ephesians 4:21).

Paul talks about 'speaking the truth *in love*' (v. 15). Love without truth is like doing heart surgery with a wet fish. But truth without love is like doing heart surgery with a hammer. We will only speak the truth effectively in the context of loving relationships.

Moreover, we don't just communicate truth by our words. We also embody truth in our lives. 'No one has ever seen God, but if we love one another, God lives in us and his love is made complete in us' (1 John 4:12). We make the invisible God visible to one another through our actions. We're to forgive 'just as in Christ God forgave you' (Ephesians 4:32). We're to love 'just as Christ loved us' (5:2). People have often told me how a Christian was there for them in a moment of loss or crisis – perhaps simply cooking a meal or holding a hand – and this helped them to see that God was there for them in their darkness.

One way we can speak the truth into people's lives is by narrating how the truth has had an impact on our own life. This personalises the truth and helps people to see how it applies today. It's also a good way to speak truth if we lack the confidence or an opening to do so in more direct ways. If, for example, someone is complaining about ill health, we might say, 'Yes, sickness can be a real struggle. When I was in hospital last year, I had to keep reminding myself that God is with us in our difficulties and he uses our suffering for our good. I needed to trust God's fatherly care.'

As we seek to support one another in change, we must ensure that we're proclaiming the gospel, not law. Law says, 'You *should not . . .* ' 'You should not speak like that.' 'You should not grumble.' 'You should not parent in that way.' Does that sound familiar? It's all true, but on its own it's not good news. For a struggling saint, these can be words of condemnation. It's true that occasionally we will need to challenge behaviour, but we must always point people to the gospel. And what the gospel says is this: '*You need not . . .* ' 'You need not get drunk because Jesus offers a better refuge.' 'You need not lose your temper because God is in control of this situation.' Sin makes promises. The gospel exposes those promises as false promises and points to God, who is bigger and better than anything sin offers. That's good news.

A community of repentance

There are some sins that thrive on secrecy. They include sins of escape – things we do when we're feeling under pressure, such as sexual fantasies, pornography, compulsive eating and addictions. They include sins of the mind – bitterness, envy, jealousy, complaining. We can become very adept at hiding these things, but hiding them feeds them. You feel bad about yourself so you eat compulsively. You eat compulsively so you feel bad about yourself. You feel unable to cope with life so you become a hero in a computer game. But your addiction makes the real world seem even harder. The fear of exposure means you withdraw from the Christian community or learn to pretend. But withdrawal and pretence cut you off from the help of the community. One thing we've learned in our church is that change often only really takes place when these sins come out into the open. It's difficult, but confession to another Christian will be a big step forward. You don't need to tell everyone! But tell someone – a mature Christian you can trust.

What should you do if someone confesses their sin to you? Speak the truth in love. Don't tell them that their sin is understandable or insignificant. That offers no comfort to people because it's a lie. But we can speak words of comfort because we can speak words of grace. So call them to repent their sin and to accept by faith the forgiveness that God offers. 'You are guilty, but Christ has borne your guilt. You deserve God's judgement, but Christ has borne your judgement.' This is true comfort. Embody that forgiveness in your ongoing acceptance and love, but accept people with God's agenda for change. Be proactive about offering accountability. That means asking the question! Ask them how they're getting on; ask them whether they've sinned again. Above all, point them to the grace and glory of Christ. Explore, if you can, the lies and desires that lead to their sinful behaviour. Together, you may be able to discern the truths that they need to turn to and the idolatrous desires they need to turn from. But don't worry if you can't do this kind of analysis. It's enough to show love to people and speak 'the truth that is Jesus'.

'Brothers and sisters, if someone is caught in a sin, you who live by the Spirit should restore that person gently,' says Paul in Galatians 6:1–2. 'But watch yourselves, or you also may be tempted. Carry each other's burdens, and in this way you will fulfil the law of

Christ. Most of the time that means being there for people, being willing to talk, weeping with them in their pain, modelling God's grace to them. Occasionally it may be appropriate to challenge their behaviour (Colossians 1:28; 3:16; 2 Timothy 4:2; Titus 2:15). Challenge people:

- **reluctantly** only challenge persistent patterns of behaviour – don't find fault at every turn
- **cautiously** you may not know the full picture
- **humbly** you're just as much a sinner as they are – even if you don't struggle with their particular problem
- **wisely** your aim is that they become more like Christ – not for them to become like you or follow your agenda
- **patiently** change takes a lifetime – as you know from your own experience.

A community of grace

We can only be communities of change if we're communities of grace. That means being open and honest about our own struggles. And it means accepting one another just as Christ accepted us. It means that I don't pose as a good person. Instead, I portray myself as I truly am: a sinner who constantly receives grace from Christ. We rejoice in being a group of messy people, led by messy people. For, to paraphrase the first beatitude, 'Blessed are the broken people for theirs is the kingdom of heaven' (Matthew 5:3). The alternative is to be a church in which everyone is pretending – where people have problems, but the culture doesn't allow them to be open about those problems. Churches like that are neat and respectable, but they're not places where growth takes place or where grace is treasured.

In John 4, Jesus meets a Samaritan woman at a well at midday. Mad dogs and Englishmen go out in the midday sun, sang Noël Coward. Everyone else gathered water in the cool of early morning, but she comes at midday. It's to avoid the rest of the community because of the shame she feels. After she meets Jesus, however, she runs to the community she's been avoiding and says, 'Come, see a man who told me everything I've ever done' (v. 29). The good news for her was that Jesus knew her sin and shame, and still he offered her living water! She no longer had to hide. It's this testimony that draws the townspeople to Jesus. We can confess our sin to one another because there's no longer any need to hide. Grace sets us free.

Why don't we look to one another for support in change? Why don't we open up to others? Why do we avoid messy relationships? No doubt there are many reasons. We're too busy, too independent, too fearful, too self-absorbed. But if we truly believe that Jesus has given us the Christian community to help us change, then we will make it a priority.

Supporting change – some FAQs

Let me close this chapter with a few pointers to those involved in supporting other people through a process of change.

What about secular counselling?

The evidence suggests people usually find that talking therapies lead to positive outcomes. Whatever the theoretical framework of the counsellor, it's helpful talking to someone who gives you their undivided attention, especially if that person is an experienced counsellor who is outside the situation. Counsellors are often able to help people develop coping strategies.

But remember, our ultimate goal is to become more like Jesus (as we saw in Chapter 1) and only the gospel can bring about that kind of change. Cognitive behaviour therapy (CBT), for example, can help people to reject the lies that are shaping their behaviour, but it can't point people to 'the truth that is in Jesus'. We mustn't lose confidence in the word of God coming in the power of the Spirit of God. The Church is the context God himself was given for change. I can't solve anyone's problems, but I know a man who can! Christ, and Christ alone, is the Saviour of the world. And he's your Saviour, too, if you turn to him in faith and keep on turning to him in faith. Your problems may not disappear overnight, but God will use them to make you more like Jesus, and he will bring you safely home to glory.

What about medication?

Medication can help to alleviate the symptoms of some psychological problems. It makes life more bearable for people, so I never tell people to come off medication. It can have its own problems (such as addiction), but that's a matter for them to discuss with their doctor.

Our ultimate goal is to become like Christ. Medication can't do that, but I find it's helpful to think of it as creating a space for the gospel to get to work. Medication can moderate the extremes of a person's behaviour. That then enables them to engage with 'the truth that is Jesus'.

What about confidentiality?

My rule of thumb is to *practise* confidentiality but *not promise* confidentiality. That's because it may be appropriate in some situations to talk with your pastor or ministry leader about what someone has told you for the purposes of advice and accountability. There are a few scenarios (such as cases of abuse) in which you would have a legal requirement to tell someone, such as a safeguarding officer, so you can't promise that you won't tell anyone.

As well as practising confidentiality, it's important to establish a reputation for discretion. Here are some things not to say.

- 'I probably shouldn't say this, but . . . ' Guess what? That probably means you shouldn't say it!
- 'I'm only sharing this for prayer.' People can pray in ignorance because God is all-knowing.
- 'I do know, but I can't say.' This is just showing off about having insider knowledge. You may be making yourself look good, but it's at the expense of making other people feel like outsiders.

When should I ask for help?

As noted earlier in this chapter, we can and should have confidence in the word of God coming in the power of the Spirit of God. However, we can't have the same confidence in ourselves! We, too, are messed-up sinners with limited understanding and our own issues at play.

- Let's suppose someone has shared a big problem with you. It's OK to say, 'I need help. I don't know what to say or do.' Talk to your pastor or, if you are a pastor, talk to another who is more experienced or a professional counsellor. Tell the person involved that this is what you're doing.
- It may be that someone is leaning on you for support and it's becoming too much – the emotional demands are taking their toll. Again, it's OK to say, 'I need help.' Change is a community project and that means you don't have to do it all on your own. Find other people to share the load. Sometimes the person in need might want to relate to you and you alone. Flattering though this can be, you should resist such a situation. They're making you their saviour, and your goal is to keep turning them to Christ as Saviour. Your goal is to move them from dependence on you to dependence on Christ.

'The four Gs' for people supporting others through change

Imagine that someone has come to see me for some pastoral support. I make them a cup of tea and we sit together in my front room. They confess their sin to me and look to me for help. How many sinners are there in that room?

The answer, of course, is two. There's the person who has just confessed their sin, but there's also me! I want to respond in a gospel-centred way by pointing them to Jesus, but my own deceitful desires are also at play. If I'm not careful, these will distort the process. My agenda will interfere with God's agenda.

The good news is that the gospel not only liberates sinners from sin but it also liberates the sinners who support sinners! In Chapter 5, we identified four truths – the four Gs – which liberate us from the lies that underlie our sinful behaviour.

1 God is great – so we do not have to be in control.
2 God is glorious – so we do not have to fear others.
3 God is good – so we do not have to look elsewhere.
4 God is gracious – so we do not have to prove ourselves.

Consider how these help us support people well.

God is great

If we think that we need to be in control, then we may become over-bearing. We may correct every error for fear people will go astray. We'll not give people time to change or space to disagree. But when we embrace the truth that God is great, our pastoral care can be more relaxed and patient. We'll not feel the need to sort everything out in one go. The person's future is in God's hands, not mine.

God is glorious

If we're being shaped by other people's opinions, then we may be reluctant to speak the truth in case people dislike us or reject us. Or we may treat 'unrespectable' sins more seriously than other sins because respectability rather than holiness is what matters to us. But when we embrace the truth that God is glorious, we'll be free to speak the truth people *need* to hear, not just what they *want* to hear. Only then will we be truly free to serve them in love. Plus, we can be open and vulnerable because we have God's approval in Christ.

God is good

If we're not finding satisfaction in Christ, then we may be reluctant to get involved in other people's mess. Or we may start to view supporting people as a burden. But when we embrace the truth that God is good and so look for joy in him, we'll serve with more enthusiasm. We'll be generous with our time and our emotional energy.

God is gracious

If we're concerned about proving ourselves, then we may take on more than we can bear. We'll take criticism badly because our identity is tied up with our achievements rather than what Christ has achieved on our behalf. Or we may make others feel guilty as we impose high expectations on them. But when we embrace the truth that God is gracious and find our identity in Christ, our lives will be characterised by peace and rest, confidence and humility, compassion and kindness. Our concern will be with wanting to bless rather than to impress. We can be transparent and vulnerable because we won't feel the need to hide our sin. That in turn will create a context in which other people feel able to share their struggles.

Reflection #1

Here's a list of things that the New Testament says we are to do (or not do) for *one another* in church:

- be at peace with one another, forgiving, agreeing, being humble, accepting, showing forbearance, living in harmony and greeting one another with a kiss
- do not judge, lie or grumble to one another
- show hospitality to one another
- confess our sins to one another
- be kind, concerned, devoted, serving and doing good to one another
- instruct and teach one another
- admonish, exhort and stir up one another
- comfort and encourage one another.[4]

Which do you think that you are good at and not so good at? Which do you think your church is good at and not so good at? What stops you doing more 'one anothering'?

---

4 Mark 9:50; John 13:34–35; Romans 12:10, 16; 14:13; 15:5, 7, 14; 16:16; 1 Corinthians 12:25; 2 Corinthians 13:11–12; Galatians 5:13; Ephesians 4:2, 32; 5:19, 21; Colossians 3:9, 13, 16; 1 Thessalonians 4:18; 5:11, 15; Hebrews 3:13; 10:24–25; James 5:9, 16; 1 Peter 4:8–10; 5:5, 14.

Reflection #2

Think of three people in your church or home group. Identify one way you could bless them this week by doing something to help them, saying something encouraging or giving them a gift.

Change project

Question 9: How can we support one another in change?

What relationships do you currently have that help you to change?

What opportunities do you currently have to help others to change?

What stops you having change-orientated relationships?

- 'I'm too busy' Are you busy because you feel the need to be in control or on top of things? To prove yourself? Get the most from life? To earn the approval of others?
- 'I don't need help' Do you think, 'I don't like to trouble others' or 'I don't want to be dependent on others'?
- 'I'm afraid of what might happen' Do you avoid close relationships because they might get messy? Because you fear being vulnerable or exposed?
- 'I've got enough problems of my own' Do you think mainly about what other Christians can do for you? Are most of your conversations with Christians about you?

Do any of these statements apply to you? What do they reveal about your attitude to God? What are the lies they express? What is the truth to which you need to turn?

Is your church or small group a community of grace?

- Are people open about their sin or is there a culture of pretending?
- Is community life messy or sanitised?
- Are broken people attracted to your community or do they feel out of place?
- Is conflict out in the open or is it suppressed?
- Are forgiveness and reconciliation actively pursued or is conflict ignored?
- Do you continually return to the cross in your conversation, prayers and praise?

How can you make your Christian friendships more change-orientated?

Do you have Christian friendships that are not change-orientated? Think about a first move you could make to start helping one another to change. For example, you could:

- talk about your own struggles with sin
- suggest that you read the Bible and pray together
- ask someone about their relationship with God or their change project
- message someone when you're struggling with temptation.

Think about practical ways you can help, or be helped, to avoid temptation or situations that reinforce sinful desires. You may need help:

- **In particular places** I have a friend who's a recovering alcoholic. When he wants to watch football in the pub, we make sure there's someone who'll go with him.
- **At particular times** I'm more vulnerable to temptation when my family are away, so I try to arrange to spend time with others.

Write one thing you're going to do to ensure that you are more supported by other Christians, and one thing you're going to do to provide support for other Christians.

10

Are you ready for a lifetime of daily change?

There's a lot of talk about freedom of choice. Whether it's what's on supermarket shelves, health provision, sexual orientation and gender or even the fate of unborn children, our culture wants freedom of choice. But from a Christian perspective, freedom of choice in one important sense is a myth. Human beings are not free to choose: they're slaves to their sinful desires. We can choose between white and brown bread, full-fat and semi-skimmed milk, but we can't choose to live holy lives. We're not free to be the people we should be or even the people we want to be. We're controlled by whatever has captured our hearts, and 'Those who live according to the flesh have their minds set on what the flesh desires' (Romans 8:5).

Free to choose, free to struggle

But Jesus sets us free. He sets us free by giving us another desire: the desire for God. We still do what we want, but Jesus gives us a new desire, so now we want to serve God. He does this by putting his Spirit in our hearts: 'those who live in accordance with the Spirit have their minds set on what the Spirit desires' (Romans 8:5).

So now Christians can choose. The old desires still linger, but the Spirit has placed this new desire in our hearts. Each day we're faced with a choice between these two desires: the deceitful desire for sin and the Spirit-inspired desire for God. Elyse Fitzpatrick says, 'Before [a person] was saved there was only one possible outcome in every choice: he was going to sin. But now that he has a new heart, there are two possibilities. He can sin or he can not sin, freely choosing according to his desires.'[1]

The Bible describes this struggle between our old sinful desires and our new Spirit-inspired desires as a war. And the battleground is our hearts. 'Dear friends, I urge you, as foreigners and exiles, to abstain from sinful desires, which wage war against your soul' (1 Peter 2:11). 'For the flesh desires what is contrary to the Spirit, and the Spirit what is contrary to the flesh. They are in conflict with each other, so that you are not to do whatever you want' (Galatians 5:17). When we want to follow our sinful desires, the Spirit opposes us. When we want to follow our Spirit-inspired desire for holiness, the flesh opposes us. We never quite do what we want for our flesh stops us serving wholeheartedly and the Spirit stops us sinning wholeheartedly. No wonder we experience life as a battle! This is why Paul adds, 'Let us not become weary in doing good, for at the proper time we will reap a harvest if we do not give up' (6:9). The question we need to ask ourselves is, *are you ready for a lifetime of daily change?*

A lifetime of daily struggle

Change is a lifetime task

Change isn't a one-off event. Sanctification is progressive. It's a marathon, not a sprint. Christians are called to a lifetime of change as the habits and thought processes of sin are not easily unlearnt. There are few quick fixes. We'll never be perfect in this life, but we can always and should always be changing.

'We are God's handiwork,' says Paul in Ephesians 2:10. It is as though, suggests Horatius Bonar, God is sculpting us, like statues, into the image of his Son. Except, he adds, that we are not inanimate marble. That would be a simple task, but the remoulding of the soul is unspeakably more difficult. The influences at work – internal and external, spiritual and physical – are numerous. Yet,

---

1 Elyse Fitzpatrick, *Idols of the Heart: Learning to long for God alone* (Phillipsburg, NJ: P&R Publishing, 2001), p. 147.

over the course of a lifetime, without violating our will and yet without fail, God fashions us into the image of his Son.[2]

Sometimes people are dramatically changed and one area of struggle disappears almost overnight. But this is rare. Even when it happens, plenty of other areas of struggle remain. Most of us find change a slow battle. Although the analysis can be quick, change is slow. We mustn't confuse the two. Understanding the lies and desires behind our sin doesn't mean that the problem is solved. Now I simply know where the fight is taking place. I know where to deploy my forces. I know the truth I need to embrace. But the struggle to believe that truth continues.

Change is a daily task

Faith and repentance are daily disciplines. Turning from sinful desires in faith today doesn't mean that the problem will have gone away tomorrow. I may well find myself having to turn from my sinful desires today, tomorrow and day by day after that. I may realise that I crave the approval of certain people, so they've become an idol in my heart. I may determine to fear God more than I fear those people. But it will still be a daily struggle to remember that God is bigger than they are. I may realise that my identity is defined by the clothes I wear rather than my relationship with Christ. So I may cut up my store cards and cancel my catalogues, but tomorrow, when I walk past a shop window, the struggle in my heart will flare up again.

> The gospel is so foolish (according to my natural wisdom), so scandalous (according to my conscience), and so incredible (according to my timid heart), that it is a daily battle to believe the full scope of it as I should. There is simply no other way to compete with the forebodings of my conscience, the condemnings of my heart, and the lies of the world and the

---

2 Horatius Bonar, *God's Way of Holiness* (Darlington: Evangelical Press, 1979), pp. 5–6.

Devil than to overwhelm such things with daily rehearsings of the gospel.[3]

The battle for holiness is made up of what Horatius Bonar calls 'daily littles'.[4] It's not given to many of us to make life-and-death decisions for our Saviour. Not many will be faced with a choice between recanting or being martyred. No, for us the battle is made up of a thousand little moments: choices between self and service. We'll not fall when we face the threat of death, but may well do when we face the reality of a traffic jam. It's too easy to imagine that we are strong Christians who would stand firm in the face of persecution, but every day we let sinful desires control us. We imagine ourselves winning the great battles when, all the time, we're losing the 'daily littles'. But the daily littles *are* the stuff of battles. Bonar says:

> The Christian life is a great thing, one of the greatest things on earth. Made up of daily littles, it is yet in itself not a little thing, but in so far as it is truly lived . . . is noble throughout – a part of that great whole, in which and by which is to be made known to the principalities and power in heavenly places the manifold wisdom of God (Eph. 3:10).[5]

We must always be on a war footing. Imagine a soldier in the thick of battle who decides that today is his day off. He unfolds his deckchair, puts on his sunglasses, gets out his book and sits in the sun reading. He wouldn't last long! 'Be alert and of sober mind. Your enemy the devil prowls around like a roaring lion looking for someone to devour. Resist him, standing firm in the faith, because you know that the family of believers throughout the world is undergoing the same kind of sufferings' (1 Peter 5:8–9). We need

---

3   Milton Vincent, *A Gospel Primer for Christians* (2006), p. 14, citing 1 Corinthians 1:21, 23; 1 John 3:19–20; 2 Corinthians 4:4, available at: https://tinyurl.com/4hs8yzlu.

4   Horatius Bonar, *God's Way of Holiness* (Darlington: Evangelical Press, 1979), p. 127.

5   Bonar, *God's Way of Holiness*, pp. 5–6.

to be in a constant state of alert because our enemy is in a constant state of attack (Ephesians 6:14–17). John Flavel says:

> Keeping the heart is a constant work. Keeping the heart is a work that is never done until life is over. There is no time or condition in the life of a Christian which can allow a let-up of this work . . . A few minutes break from the task of watching their hearts cost David and Peter many a sad day and night. It is the most important business of a Christian's life.[6]

There are amazing stories of Japanese soldiers who defended remote islands long after the Second World War had ended. People turned up in the 1950s to find them in a state of battle readiness because, somehow, the news of peace had never got through. Christians can suffer the opposite problem. Some Christians seem not to have received the news that the war's started. They act as though we're living in peacetime when, in fact, we're at war with the world, the flesh and the devil.

We've seen how we're changed by faith. But this is not passive or inactive faith. The Wesleyan and old Keswick traditions also emphasised the centrality of faith in sanctification, but often in unhelpful ways. The Wesleyan tradition taught people to look for a crisis moment akin to conversion, which brought you into a state of 'entire sanctification'. In the Keswick tradition, faith was understood as reliance on Christ that brought you into the 'higher life' in which sin, while not eradicated, was suppressed by the Spirit.[7]

Biblical change differs significantly from these two approaches. First, sanctifying faith is a repeated act as, day by day, we affirm our new identity in Christ and find greater delight in God than in sin. Sanctification may involve some crisis experiences in which we make leaps forward, but it remains a lifelong process.

Second, sanctifying faith is hard, disciplined work: 'Make every effort to live in peace with everyone and to be holy; without

---

6 Adapted from John Flavel, *Keeping the Heart* (Fearn, Ross-shire: Christian Heritage, 1999), p. 20.

7 See David Bebbington, *Holiness in Nineteenth-century England* (Carlisle: Paternoster, 2000).

holiness no one will see the Lord' (Hebrews 12:14). It involves the effort, with the help of the Spirit, of affirming the greatness and goodness of God. It's an effort to keep believing when the world, the flesh and the devil whisper lies that contradict the truth. Such faith is reinforced by the means of grace, which we should use in a disciplined way. We aren't talking about passive faith that waits on God for a special experience to release us from struggle. Passive faith and legalistic works are not the only options! The biblical option is 'the fight of faith'[8] – an active battle to exercise of faith in reliance on the Holy Spirit. It's about faith driving a thousand acts of the will, making daily choices to see past the lies of sin. Change is a lifelong, daily struggle.

A lifetime of hope

Change may be a lifelong, daily struggle, but there's plenty of reason to hope. We will reap a harvest of holiness (Galatians 6:9) and change is certain.

I can change

I can change because 'I have been crucified with Christ and I no longer live, but Christ lives in me' (2:20). Christ has broken the hold of sin over our life. It's now not inevitable that we sin. The old sinful nature has been replaced by a new nature. God has given us his Spirit, with new desires to shape our behaviour. Sin no longer defines us. Change is certain because of Christ's work for us and the Spirit's work in us.

This means that change is always possible. There's no sin in which we need be trapped. There's no area of life that we cannot change. You may have been committing the same sin over and over again for many years. Change will not be easy. Sin is habit-forming – both habits of behaviour and habits of thinking. But change *is* possible. For, just as sin is habit-forming, so is holiness. You may gradually find yourself struggling less with certain sins. Speaking

---

8 J. C. Ryle, *Holiness: Its nature, hindrances, difficulties and roots* (Cambridge: James Clarke, 1956), pp. 57–60.

truth to yourself day by day will create new habits of thinking. Every time you resist temptation, you weaken the influence of your sinful desires.

Christians need never plateau. Many Christians grew quickly when they first converted. They were full of enthusiasm and their lives changed dramatically. Then, after a while, they settled down into a routine. All the public, embarrassing sins have been swept away, but now there's little real growth. If change could be represented as a line on a graph, then we'd see that their line has gone flat. Their behaviour has changed, but their hearts go unchallenged. It needn't be this way. Change is always possible.

Other Christians worry that they're not growing when they are. Often, growth in grace comes with an increasing awareness of our sin.[9] We see the dirt in our hearts all the more as we move towards the light of God. Like a computer game in which you progress up through the levels, so it is with sanctification. Level one are the obvious, clear sins that others see in us. By level ten, we're becoming aware of subtle and deceitful desires embedded in our hearts. John Newton wrote, 'The growth of a believer is not like a mushroom but like an oak, which increases slowly but surely. Many suns, showers and frosts pass upon it before it comes to perfection; and in winter, when it seems dead, it is gathering strength at the root.'[10]

We need to look both back and forwards. When we look back to what we were, we should feel encouraged by how we've changed. When we look forwards to what we will be, we should feel excited at the prospect of further change. If we get the tension wrong between the 'already' and 'not yet', we'll either have unrealistic expectations of perfection or give up in defeat.[11]

Maybe you've tried changing with a new determination as you've read this book, but still you've fallen back into sin. Please don't give up. Let me summarise what we've seen about change. Is there something you're missing?

---

9   J. I. Packer, *A Passion for Holiness* (Wheaton, IL: Crossway, 1992), pp. 156 and 221.

10 John Newton, *The Works of John Newton* (Edinburgh: Banner of Truth, 1985), Vol. 2, p. 141.

11 Sinclair B. Ferguson, *The Holy Spirit* (Leicester: IVP, 1996), p. 149.

1 Keep returning to the cross to see your sin cancelled and disarmed, so you draw near to God in full assurance of welcome.
2 Keep looking to God instead of sin for satisfaction, focusing on the four liberating truths of God's greatness, glory, goodness and grace ('the four Gs').
3 Cut off, throw off, put off, kill off everything that might strengthen or provoke sinful desires.
4 Bring sin into the light through regular accountability to another Christian.

If you resist doing these four things – and we often resist numbers 3 and 4 – it's a sign that you still treasure sin in your heart and sin is still more important to you than God. Turn to God in repentance, reflect on sin's consequences, meditate on the all-surpassing glory of Christ, beg God to give you a love for him that eclipses your love for sin. And then, perhaps ask a trusted Christian to walk alongside you through change.

I will change

Paul says that those who sow to the Spirit 'will reap eternal life', and 'we will reap a harvest if we do not give up' (Galatians 6:8–9). Change may take a lifetime, but it only takes one lifetime. The process of change will come to an end. One day we will be trans-formed, perfected and glorified. Not a day goes by but we feel the burden of our struggle with sin. But that struggle will come to an end and our burden will be lifted.

The Mississippi River twists and turns as it makes it way to the sea. At times, it flows north, away from the coast. But inexorably and inevitably, its water reaches the sea. Sometimes Christians can flow away from God, but still we move downstream towards the ocean of his love. God never fails: 'I am sure of this, that he who began a good work in you will bring it to completion at the day of Jesus Christ' (Philippians 1:6, ESV).

God doesn't perfect us at our death or Christ's return with a wave of a magic wand. It's the culmination of the process of sanctification in which you're currently engaged. Change takes as we see the glory of God. At present, we see his glory only partially in his word, 'But we know that when he appears, we shall be like him, for we shall see him as he is' (1 John 3:2). What perfects us is that full vision of God's glory. When faith gives way to sight, when we see the glorious greatness and goodness of God in Christ, all desire for sin will evaporate. When we grasp the full extent of God's grace, all our affections will be his for ever. In the meantime, 'All who have this hope in him purify themselves, just as he is pure' (v. 3).

A lifetime of grace

I am a sinner

Change is a lifetime of daily struggle that will come to end. But, in the meantime, it's a struggle. Often we lose the battle with temptation. Sin may no longer define our identity, but it's still a feature of our lives.

We can't expect to stop sinning in this life. We shouldn't hold out this hope to people, nor claim it for ourselves. Some people in the history of the Church, including the great John Wesley,[12] have believed that we can achieve a state of 'sinless perfection' in this life.[13] The universal experience of Christians suggests otherwise. Indeed, Wesley never claimed perfection for himself, perhaps because he knew his own heart too well. A great Victorian preacher, Charles Spurgeon, is reported to have heard someone declare that they had achieved sinless perfection. Spurgeon said nothing at the time but, at breakfast the next morning, he poured a jug of milk over the man to test his claim. It soon proved false![14]

The Bible also refutes sinless perfection in this life: 'If we claim to be without sin, we deceive ourselves and the truth is not in us'

---

12 John Wesley, 'Sermon 34: Christian Perfection', *Forty-Four Sermons* (London: Epworth Press, 1944), pp. 457–80.

13 See Donald Alexander (ed.), *Christian Spirituality: Five views of sanctification* (Downers Grove, IL: InterVarsity Press, 1988).

14 There are various versions of this story. See R. Paul Stevens and Michael Green, *Living the Story: Biblical spirituality for everyday Christians* (Grand Rapids, MI: Eerdmans, 2003), p. 141 and Charles H. Spurgeon, *The Early Years* (Edinburgh: Banner of Truth, 1962), pp. 228–30.

(1:8). Such perfectionism has to employ a sub-biblical definition of sin as merely wilful acts of transgression. Wesley thought perfected Christians could still commit involuntary mistakes or ignorant errors, but not intentional transgressions. Sin is much more than sinful acts. It's the in-built bias against God that has corrupted our thoughts, desires and will,[15] making us subject to compulsive behaviour and causing us to suppress the truth (Romans 1:18–32). Actions that look involuntary or ignorant actually reflect our deep-seated corruption. Assuming perfection is the sort of pride that leads to a fall. If we think we've risen above the daily struggle with sin, then the devil may move in for the kill.

But this creates an apparent discrepancy. Sin is never inevitable because Jesus has broken the power of sin (1 John 3:4–6). Yet it is inevitable because I know I'll continue to sin in this life (1:9 – 2:2). The truth is that I'm not bound to commit any particular sin, but I still make choices to sin because my desires have not yet been completely transformed: 'There remains in a regenerate man a smouldering cinder of evil,' says John Calvin, 'from which desires continually leap forth to allure and spur him to commit sin.'[16] My desires have not been completely transformed because I've not yet seen God as he truly is. My faith is not strong enough to grasp what one day I'll see – the true greatness and goodness of God. It's only when God appears and we see him as he is that we shall be like him (3:2).

I am righteous

'If we claim to be without sin, we deceive ourselves and the truth is not in us,' says the Apostle John. But, he continues, 'If we confess our sins, he is faithful and just and will forgive us our sins and purify us from all unrighteousness' (1:9). I've written this book that you might not sin. We can change because of Christ's work for us and the Spirit's work in us. But in this life we'll still sin. I'm still a sinner and I'll be a sinner until the day I die or Christ returns. But

15 John Calvin, *Institutes of the Christian Religion*, ed. John T. McNeill, trans. Ford Lewis Battles (Philadelphia, PA/London: Westminster/SCM Press, 1961), 3.3.10.

16 Calvin, *Institutes of the Christian Religion*, 3.3.10.

God is also gracious and he'll be gracious until the day I die and for all eternity. Christ has died for my sins and his death is effective until the day I die and for all eternity. I'm a sinner, but I'm a justified sinner. The Reformers had a Latin phrase to capture this truth: semper peccator, semper iustus – 'always a sinner, always justified'. I still sin but, in Christ, God declares me to be righteous here and now.

So we need not and should not despair. If we think of ourselves only as failed sinners, then we may feel disqualified from Christian service and settle for a compromised life. But you are a justified saint, equipped for battle, capable of adventurous, risky discipleship on the frontline of God's kingdom.

Sin is never the last word for the children of God; grace always has the last word. If we confess our sins to God, he is faithful. He'll keep his promise to forgive. Jesus said of the Communion wine, 'This is my blood of the new covenant, which is poured out for many for the forgiveness of sins' (Matthew 26:28). God is faithful to that covenant:

> My dear children, I write this to you so that you will not sin.
> But if anybody does sin, we have an advocate with the Father
> – Jesus Christ, the Righteous One. He is the atoning sacrifice
> for our sins, and not only for ours but also for the sins of the
> whole world.
> (1 John 2:1–2)

So there is hope for change. That hope is not in counsellors or methodologies or rules. Our hope is a great and gracious Saviour who has broken the power of sin and placed his life-giving Spirit in our hearts. He calls us to look beyond the lies of sin to the glory of God. He calls us to faith in a God, who is bigger and better than anything sin offers. He calls us to turn in repentance from the idolatrous desires of our hearts that enslave and corrode to find true and lasting joy in God. Our gracious Saviour, who died for us 'while we were God's enemies', invites us to 'approach God's throne of grace with confidence, so that we may receive mercy and find grace to help us in our time of need' (Romans 5:10; Hebrews 4:16).

Reflection #1

Here's a summary of what we've seen in this chapter.

- Change is a lifetime task.
- Change is a daily task.
- I can change.
- I will change.
- I am a sinner.
- I am righteous.

Think about each of these truths in turn. What happens if you *don't* believe these truths? How would you behave? Can you see any signs of this behaviour in your life?

Reflection #2

The love of God to us, and our love to Him, work together for producing holiness. Terror accomplishes no real obedience . . . Only the certainty of love, forgiving love, can do this. It is this certainty that melts the heart, dissolves our chains, disburdens our shoulders, so that we stand erect, and makes us to run in the way of the divine commandments . . . Condemnation makes sin strike its roots deeper and deeper . . . No gloomy uncertainty as to God's favour can subdue one lust, or correct our crookedness of will. But the free pardon of the cross uproots sin, and withers all its branches . . . "All divine life, and all precious fruits of it – pardon, peace, and holiness – spring from the cross . . . All fancied sanctification which does not arise wholly from the blood of the cross is nothing better than Pharisaism . . . If we would be holy, we must get to the cross, and dwell there; or else, despite all our labour, diligence, fasting, praying and good works, we shall be devoid of real sanctification" . . . The secret of a believer's holy walk is his continual return to the blood of the cross, and his daily communion with a crucified and risen Lord.[17]

Change project

Question 10: Are you ready for a lifetime of daily change?

Are you hoping for instant change?

Think about your change project.

- Are you expecting a solution that will make your struggles go away?
- Have you ever thought that you had it 'solved' or 'sorted' it in the past?
- Are you hoping that you can stop working on it?
- Are you ready for a daily struggle?

⇨ *You may need to be more realistic about sin in your heart.*

Are you frustrated by your lack of change?

- Do you feel like you've reached a plateau in your Christian life?
- Are you discouraged by your lack of change?
- Do you feel like you're going backwards?
- In the past, have you focused on a behaviour change rather than a heart change?
- How have you changed in the past year? In the past five years?

⇨ *You may need to have more confidence in God's work in your life.*

---

17 Horatius Bonar, *The Everlasting Righteousness* (London: James Nisbet, 1873), pp. 183–9, citing John Berridge, modernised.

What do you do when you sin?

When you sin, do you feel:

- that God loves you less
- that God blesses you less
- like you need to make it up to God
- disqualified from Christian service?

None of these statements is true. God's love is constant – he doesn't love us less or bless us less when we sin. After all, Jesus died for us when we were sinners and enemies of God (Romans 5:6–10). We need not and cannot make it up to God. Christ paid the price of our sin in full on the cross.

⇨ *You may need to have more confidence in God's grace and Christ's finished work.*

Write one truth that you need to remember as you face a lifetime of daily change.

Review your change project

Look back over what you've written at the end of each chapter.

- What have you learned about yourself?
- What have you learned about God?
- What have you learned about change?
- What have you started doing or thinking?
- What do you still need to do or think?

Further reading

Beeke, Joel R. and Barrett, Michael P. V., *A Radical, Comprehensive Call to Holiness* (Fearn, Ross-shire: Mentor, 2021)

Bridges, Jerry, *The Discipline of Grace: God's role and our role in the pursuit of holiness* (Colorado Springs, CO: NavPress, 1994)

Bridges, Jerry, *The Pursuit of Holiness* (Colorado Springs, CO: NavPress, 1978)

Chester, Tim, *Captured by a Better Vision: Living porn-free* (Nottingham: IVP, 2010)

Chester, Tim, *Enjoying God: Experience the power and love of God in everyday life* (Epsom: The Good Book Company, 2018)

Ferguson, Sinclair B., *Devoted to God: Blueprints for sanctification* (Edinburgh: Banner of Truth, 2016)

Fitzpatrick, Elyse, *Idols of the Heart: Learning to long for God alone* (Phillipsburg, NJ: P&R Publishing, 2001)

Kellemen, Robert W., *Gospel-centered Counseling: How Christ changes lives* (Grand Rapids, MI: Zondervan, 2014)

Lane, Timothy S. and Tripp, Paul David, *How People Change* (Greensboro, NC: New Growth Press, 2007)

Mahaney, C. J., *Living the Cross Centered Life: Keeping the gospel the main thing* (Colorado Springs, CO: Multnomah, 2002)

Millar, J. Gary, *Changed into His Likeness: A biblical theology of personal transformation* (London: IVP, 2021)

Owen, John, *Overcoming Sin and Temptation* (Wheaton, IL: Crossway, 2006)

Packer, J. I., *A Passion for Holiness* (Wheaton, IL: Crossway, 1992)

Piper, John, *Future Grace* (Nottingham: IVP, 1995)

Piper, John, *When I Don't Desire God: How to fight for God* (Wheaton, IL: Crossway, 2004)

Ryle, J. C., *Holiness: Its nature, hindrances, difficulties and roots* (Cambridge: James Clarke, 1956)

Thorne, Helen, *Hope in an Anxious World: 6 truths for when things feel overwhelming* (Epsom: The Good Book Company, 2021)

Thorne, Helen, *Purity Is Possible: How to live free of the fantasy trap* (Epsom: The Good Book Company, 2014)

Thorne, Helen and Midgley, Steve, *Mental Health and Your Church: A handbook for biblical care* (Epsom: The Good Book Company, 2023)

Welch, Edward T., *When People Are Big and God Is Small: Overcoming peer pressure, codependendency, and the fear of man* (Phillipsburg, NJ: P&R Publishing, 1997)

Scripture and other copyright acknowledgements

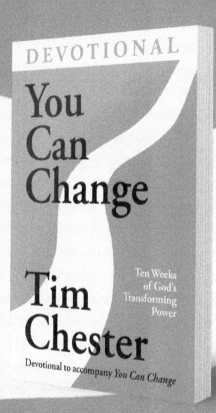